Ivan Anti_

MEDITATION

First and Last Step
From Understanding to Practice

SAMKHYA PUBLISHING LTD
London, 2020

Translated by
Milica Breber

Book cover design by:
Zoran Ignjatovic
https://ignjatoviczoran.weebly.com

Copyright © 2020 by SAMKHYA PUBLISHING LTD
All rights reserved.

ISBN: 9781795159173

CONTENT

PART ONE

The correct understanding of meditation	5
Meditation and reality	7
The nature of reality	17
The nature of energy	24
The nature of consciousness	30
Consciousness and energy reflect the nature of the absolute	34
The dimensions of existence	37
Man is a microcosm	43
We experience our timelessness through time	49
The effect of meditation and the structure of human beings - The relationship between mind and consciousness of the soul	54
Why does the mind keep deceiving us, even as it awakens us	83
Meditation and karmic maturity	91
The benefits of meditation in everyday life	101
The physics of consciousness in meditation	103
Mistakes in meditation	109
The need for a teacher in meditation	121
Meditation and death similarities and differences	127

PART TWO

The practice of meditation	139
General and specific prerequisites for meditation	141
Four dimensions of the practice of attention *vipassana* and *satipatthâna*	150
Vipassana meditation during sleep	189
Calmness of the body - how to sit	191
Calmness of the mind in meditation or contemplation	198
Rűpa-dhyânam - Four degrees of mental calmness	199
Siddhi - Powers - Consequences of meditation	226
Five degrees of actualization of the divine consciousness in existence - Arűpa-dhyânam	246
Summary of the practice of meditation	271

PART ONE

THE CORRECT UNDERSTANDING OF MEDITATION

MEDITATION AND REALITY

We shall use the term 'meditation' for one obvious reason only, which is: it is generally and widely accepted, even though the proper term for our subject is 'contemplation'. The word comes from the Latin *contemplatio*, which etymologically denotes an act of attaining a higher place (*templum*) that provides more objective and accurate vision. It is made up of the prefix con, which denotes connection or synchronization, and *templum*, a temple or sacred place where connection with the divine becomes possible, and receiving messages from the divine becomes a reality. Since it is not the external temple, but rather the inner experience, that the word 'contemplation' denotes, practically it means reaching the inner sanctuary, a state of exaltation in one's own being, that enables the merging with a higher, divine consciousness of the soul, in an attempt to harmonize with it. This brings forth the transition of consciousness to a higher level, a changing of one's own being in order to become a temple of the divine presence. With such practice comes the most objective consciousness possible in man, which serves to connect his individual consciousness with objective reality, or the divine consciousness which enables everything, and here it will be addressed as 'meditation', because that term is generally accepted, even though the word 'meditation' literally means mindful thinking. However, it is not wrong to use the word 'meditation' here, because this discussion is about making sense of contemplation. This is a meditation on contemplation, an understanding of contemplation - for only through proper understanding it can become possible.

Meditation or contemplation is a method which awakens a man to the comprehension of reality, in an accelerated way; or more precisely, a method by which the illusion of time, during which we imagine that we are something else, and not what we truly are, is removed. In meditation man harmonizes with reality. Harmonizing with reality is the lesson and the practice of meditation.

When a man is born into his physical body, he is not truly and completely born, because he still has not properly begun his existence. By being born into a physical body, the exact opposite of origin actually occurs: the limitation and collapsing into a far lower state of consciousness than the one we had before birth. Man uses birth into a physical body as an option for presence in existence. But even then, his existence does not become complete just by birth of the body itself; instead it opens new windows of opportunity for man's existence in physical reality. When it is born, the physical body is still conditioned; it has only replaced the narrow environment of the uterus with the wider environment of the world it enters. This world is far wider, and enables more movement and greater perception, but that wideness and apparent freedom of movement and action should not deceive us into thinking that with physical birth we begin to exist as a free and a self-conscious being. All the conditionality and suffering which we experience, all the conflicts and misunderstandings, are proof that we are not truly free and completely our own. They are the consequence of our lack of awareness and conditionality consequent of the wider environment.

Meditation is a method by which man becomes completely realized and present in existence, in all its dimensions, and even in physical reality - truly unconditioned and authentically himself. Only with meditation does man start to truly exist, and free himself from the illusion that he started to exist by the mere act of the physical birth, and from the illusion of the physical body. In this way, he brings consciousness of his soul, which he possessed before birth, to his existence during his physical lifetime. That is the aim of meditation. In this book, all of the details of this accomplishment will be presented.

All of life is a process of being born into the spirit, into consciousness of the soul. The act of physical birth is only the beginning; to be more accurate, it is only one phase of the long process of birth of the spirit. But why do we even bother with birth of the spirit, and with the physical process? What is the purpose of life in a physical body? It surely has to be part of some wider context. Surely the goal of meditation is also to recognize this, to get to know the purpose that surpasses our life, all of our lives. That goal cannot be shown here; it is not something which has an answer, instead we have to reach it individually, by way of self-realization. However, we can give a hint, so that the purpose of meditation and the nature of reality become a lot clearer to us. After all, were it not for a hint of this kind, no one would be inspired to meditate, as the practice of meditation often brings many temptations and renunciations to beginners.

Meditation is the act of merging consciousness of the soul, which we had before our birth, with the body; and, likewise, the soul we will have after death of the body. It is so attractive to people with mature souls: the fact that even the slightest insinuation on well-being that meditation offers, however unclear, gives enormous energy and inspiration for progress, for further practice. There are a great many meditation practitioners in the world, who do not completely understand what meditation is and what it does, but they are nonetheless fascinated by it; and then there are those few who do understand it. This is the power of the attraction of the soul. Everyone who meditates correctly realizes the purpose of meditation with experience and time, but at the beginning it is invisible. This is understandable, because it represents the change in the state of consciousness. It starts with the lower state, which does not enable a clear vision of the higher realms that become accessible to us only with disciplined practice. Those who are able to clearly see the purpose of meditation have, by perfecting the practice, automatically achieved the end result - to meditate correctly. Meditation is practiced only until its correctness is achieved; once it is achieved, it is complete, because correct meditation conveys true compatibility with reality. Therefore, every practice of meditation before that final moment is inherently imperfect. Meditation only exists as a more or less successful attempt to perfect oneself through diligence and discipline. The very moment it becomes perfect, it disappears, because it is no different from the highest divine reality, from everything which is, here and now, from the essence of existence. The meditant also disappears at that moment, because there is nothing in the world but the highest divine reality. Only it exists, and nothing more. In the same way, the meditant who upon achieving the full realization of the divine reality disappears into it, as the divine turns into itself and becomes what it is - itself. With meditation, time as an illusion disappears, and leaves open space for the truth: that man is nothing but the most supreme divine reality and its universal presence.

The highest divine reality is the source of consciousness, according to which everything that there is exists - the entire universe, and all universes.

The divine consciousness is the essence of everything, and even our essence, our soul.

All the consciousness in us comes from consciousness of the soul.

Therefore, cognition of this wider context, which goes far beyond our physical existence and all individual experiences, is brought by consciousness of our soul.

It could be said that man does not begin to exist in birth of the physical body, since he has existed before and will exist after the physical life of the body, but also that he lost his real existence in birth, and whilst in the physical body he is the most dead he could ever be. But if during his existence in a physical body, he manages to realize a full awareness of his essence, the soul (which he had had before he was born), he really will exist like he never has before. Only then, once such a man has and never loses the consciousness of his soul, will the cycle of his incarnations be interrupted, because the consciousness of his soul becomes perfectly synchronized with the divine consciousness, so it needs nothing more. It becomes incapable of forgetting its essence, no matter what form of existence it finds itself in. The method of realizing full presence of the awareness of the soul in the physical body is meditation.

This is why we state that we did not start to exist with the birth of the physical body, because we already existed before, as a soul, as part of the divine whole. By being born into a body, our consciousness becomes limited within the boundaries of an individual being, who has the illusion of separation from the whole and from his soul. Once, via meditation, we succeed, despite such restricting conditions, down-trodden by the body and physical conditionality, and use meditation in order to become aware of consciousness of our soul and make it stronger by grounding it in our body to the degree it becomes permanent and invincible, then the divine consciousness, which is the source of our soul, will truly be present in all of its aspects. It is not present in all of its possibilities while it is in itself only; it has to create the illusion of detachment from itself, and that is man's mind in his body. It must get to know itself, as itself in everything, even in forms and circumstances seemingly completely different from the divine consciousness. The illusion of something which is completely different to the omnipresent divine consciousness is man in the madness of his egocentric mind and life which contradicts nature, wholeness, other people and itself. What gives meaning to man's life is this ability to fight and come out as a winner in the battle for his soul, and to never lose this consciousness in the tug-of-war with life. That is man's tantra in this world.

The wider context of our existence can certainly be seen in everything, meditation is not even required as a tool for this; one should only make an effort to observe carefully and objectively (meditation is nothing but careful and objective self-observation, to ascertain the obvious during this process). Firstly, life itself is so complex that its complexity acts as proof that there must be something greater, far beyond what the eyes can see, much more than the physical world itself. Science shows that we, with our physical senses, are able to observe only a tiny portion of reality and of the nature that surrounds us - the proverbial 5%. The remaining 95% of nature we cannot perceive, although it exists. This much larger part of existence that we do not perceive is described by religions as 'higher worlds' and 'Kingdom Come', while mystical teachings describe them as higher dimensions. They even teach us how to train our perception to become aware of these higher dimensions; they tell us we can get out of the body to enter them. Many people experience this spontaneously but without understanding. Science notes similar phenomena; physics tells us about higher dimensions, and quantum physics tells us that the very nature of the physical world is such that our perception is conditioned and incorrect, and very limited. All that we consider to be our life and existence is placed in that limited area of our perception, in those 5%. Therefore, the logical conclusion follows that what we call 'death' belongs to that far broader, unknown area from the one we perceive and call 'life'. Hence, our existence encapsulates our physical life and our physical death. If our existence encapsulates both, it means that it overcomes both. If we have come to the point of being aware of our death, as well as our birth, then the same consciousness must have the ability to overcome them both; it must be immortal.

The wider context of our existence can also be seen in the powerful attraction we have toward things that overcome us, that are beyond. It is the higher dimension of our being that attracts us when we sacrifice ourselves for a sublime ideal, a dear person, in love for a child. With all that we always rely on what lies beyond, which exceeds the powers of our body and mind.

The complexity of life also shows and scientifically proves that behind everything there is a clear consciousness, plan and intention. Life is not a coincidence, nor can consciousness occur as a product of something unconscious. No matter how long and complex, unconscious and random processes cannot result in consciousness. In its essence, consciousness is transcendental in relation to existence and life. It is above life, yet enables all life. Life is a direct result of intelligent design. Finally, all life proves this by its own design.

One basic example is the perfect illustration. Life itself is based on the division of cells, and it is preceded by the division of DNA. The division of DNA is not possible by itself, the complex task is done by proteins. However, the code for the creation of proteins is located in the DNA. It is obvious that DNA and proteins had to be created simultaneously by some higher consciousness. Geneticists who discovered DNA claim that it could not have happened purely by evolution, it appears to have originated by way of intelligent design. This intelligence in question is a conscious intention. Since all life in the cosmos is interconnected symbiotically - it has been proved that subatomic particles, and even cells, communicate with each other constantly, even independently from time and space, while the cells of our body consciously communicate with the cosmos – this conclusively means that this consciousness is one and the same. Multi-consciousness is not an option in nature only one universal consciousness that divides itself and branches out into individual shapes and beings, perceptions and actions.

Quantum physics proves that there are higher dimensions and parallel realities. If we are aware of what quantum physics proves, then our consciousness must be above the quantum field of all the dimensions and parallel realities. Awareness is possible only if consciousness is able to surpass the dimensions and parallel realities.

All of this indicates and proves that consciousness is also our essence or soul. All scientific discoveries prove the existence of consciousness of the soul; they prove that our soul is not some set of energies which drive our body, or a bunch of psychic impressions which appear and disappear with the body, but our soul is the same transcendental consciousness which discovers and enables existence itself, life itself, and all of the manifested world. The scientific evidence in favour of the soul is our awareness of the manifested world.

According to this, our soul has divine characteristics. The truth about our soul is that it is nothing but an individual emanation of the divine consciousness, the consciousness which can enable everything, which is one and the same in everything. The fact that we can be aware of everything, of all of existence, as well as experience our unity with the existence to the same degree that we possess awareness of our soul, and our capability of being true to ourselves and to our essence, proves that. The conscious unity of the soul and existence, we experience as love. That is why we find love so attractive that we dedicate our entire lives in hopes of finding it.

Travelling along this path, we have found the answer to our question: what is the purpose of life? It represents the manifestation of the divine consciousness, albeit a tiny part in the grand game of life, which goes beyond the time of our physical birth and our physical death, and is far greater than our physical existence. We can anticipate this just by looking at the stars. Something moves us deep inside and we feel happy. It is a consequence of the touch of our tiny individual consciousness with a far greater consciousness of our soul, with the divine consciousness which enables everything. That divine consciousness is the cosmos we can see and in which we exist. The stars are only elementary particles of it. The awareness of that invariably causes ecstasy. However, real ecstasy will follow once we learn that the only reason for the existence of the cosmos is to become aware of it. It is for the conscious subject. In this case, man. Meditation is his road to perfection in order to become a conscious subject of the entire objective existence, the cosmos.

Now that we have come to the point of our essence or soul being the divine consciousness which enables everything, what is the purpose of meditation, and how does it work?

In meditation, the process which happens on a large scale in the cosmos is repeated on a small scale, in our individual existence. It boils down to the harmonization between the individual and the absolute. When, during meditation, we, successfully, consciously and intentionally, repeat to ourselves the things that keep happening on the cosmic macro plan, then we have come to the point of realization of the divine consciousness which enables everything, and we have attained the final purpose of existence: awareness. When we become aware of our soul, of ourselves, we become aware of the divine consciousness, of the whole. Practically, we can say that with meditation we become aware of that which surpasses our physical life, we reach the awareness of the soul which we had had prior to physical birth and which we will have after physical death, we surpass time and unite the divine consciousness in ourselves. In this way, we realize the presence of the divine consciousness in existence, here and now. No more, no less, this is the purpose of meditation.

THE NATURE OF REALITY

To be able to understand how large-scale events are automatically copied in the small-scale plan, which happens in us during the meditative process, we need to understand all the steps of meditation by comprehending the nature of reality first.

In order to describe the nature of reality, we need to start from the most general and primary source of existence. Here, we shall name it, for reasons of simplicity, the Absolute.

The nature of the Absolute is an integral part of the experience of spirituality in people from the earliest times; it brought about the idea of God, or the divine origin as the foundation of existence and life. In most areas of spirituality, it has been degraded and adjusted to fit the mental images of the myriad of gods, for mass consumption and to suit the everyday needs of people; but in esoteric schools, this idea has been preserved in its much purer form as the principle of the unmanifested void. In the West and in esoteric Christianity, it can be found in apophatic theology, which speaks of God who cannot be known, and in the East as the void or sunyata in Buddhism.

The nature of the Absolute has always been visually expressed in the form of a circle or a sphere. The circle shows infinity, which cannot be defined, and which has neither a beginning nor an end, and is therefore timeless, but yet again present in its entirety. That is the true nature of existence; it is within its essence one with the whole and timeless. There is nothing separated by itself or for itself.

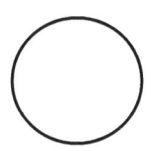

However, in such an Absolute, there is a paradox: even though by its nature it cannot be different, and as such it cannot exist, the void cannot exist; if it wants to exist, it must manifest itself in space and time. Such manifestation of the Absolute is awareness of itself. Absolute as everything-that-is is expressed as everything-that-can-be. Through everything-that-can-be the Absolute experiences consciousness of itself and all of its possibilities and aspects. When the Absolute is manifested, as in overall existence, it does not lose its absolute nature, because existence is no different from the Absolute. That means that existence is not substantial either, real in itself; it, too, represents the very unconditionality of the void, which is the essential characteristic of the Absolute. Existence and unconditionality of the void are one and the same, because nothing is possible except for the Absolute.

To emphasize what has been said: all of the manifested cosmos and all of existence is actually the awareness of the Absolute of its own nature, of itself. Existence as awareness of itself expresses that consciousness through all possible forms of existence, from subatomic particles and cells to all living beings. All of these possess the consciousness of themselves, including the events which are also aware of themselves. Through all beings and all existence and events, the Absolute actualizes consciousness of itself, as itself. All of existence, from minerals, plants and animals to people, is nothing but a spectrum of all possible forms of perception and cognition. This perception is at the heart of all evolution and development, of all of life, and the reason for all events.

How does the Absolute manage to accomplish this? How does it manifest?

Since it is timeless and spaceless, it can be manifested in a single way only: as its direct opposite.

The opposite of the Absolute is a point. Here, we will call that point the 'divine particle'. Euclid defined this point according to all the characteristics of the Absolute. And he was right. *The point or 'divine particle' contains within itself all of the properties of the Absolute, and its only feature is that it is timeless and spaceless.*[1] So we get a circle with a point, a well-known solar symbol, the source of light, consciousness and life.

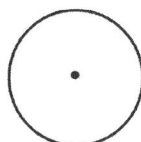

How is that point or 'divine particle' manifested, if it itself is timeless and spaceless?

It's actually really simple. However small, it is still the Absolute, and *it constantly has to keep expressing its Absolute nature* by manifesting itself in the form of the cosmos; it vibrates in all possible ways, not only much faster that the speed of light, *but currently, momentarily, in all possible ways, it is in all positions possible for existence.* In absolutely all positions. Instantly. More accurately: timelessly.

In conclusion, there are no multitude of particles and elements in nature. There is only that single point, the reflection of the Absolute, 'he 'divine particle' which currently

---

[1] The term used here, 'divine particle', has nothing in common with the book: "The God Particle", 1993, written by Leon M. Lederman and Dick Teresi. This is mainstream science. The 'divine particle' in question here corresponds with the point in Euclidean geometry, which has no dimensional properties, but rather divine characteristics.

vibrates, and those vibrations constitute all possible existence.

When something is moving fast, like when we spin a burning torch very quickly, we see the spin forming a circle. This is similar to the fast vibrations of pixels on a computer screen, which we see as a stable image; photons vibrate so fast that our limited and slow observation perceives it as a colour or solid object. The same is true for all the shapes of existence, from subatomic particles to atoms, molecules and all physical objects which we see in nature. **They are all the projection of vibration of that one and only 'divine particle' which is moving, not with speed much faster than the speed of light, but instantly.**

Since that 'divine particle' is timeless and spaceless, it is not conditioned by space and time in its movement and manifestation.

Since the Absolute itself is timeless and spaceless, it is enough that only one point is a reflection of its opposite. It would be even more accurate to say that *another particle or point is not an option, because in the Absolute there is nothing else*, only it exists and nothing else can, nothing is possible outside of it. Otherwise, it would not be the Absolute. In addition, within itself there is neither space nor time. This is why that single point can, actually must, be in all possible positions, to instantly create and sustain all shapes of existence. That point or 'divine particle' is the Absolute itself, which manifests itself into everything.

The vibrations of the 'divine particle' are expanding and becoming more complex following the principle of simplicity, which means they are expanding *in accordance with the laws of fractal geometry and golden section* on which all physical laws are based, as well as life itself.

The expansion of frequencies of energy in the form of fractals modifies space and is based on mutual crossing under angles. These angles determine the size of space and all events. This is how numbers in nature occur. Actually, there is only one number, the number one, and its opposite, zero, but that is nothing but the point and circle, the basic and original manifestation of the Absolute, which in the same way is manifested like everything else. All other numbers are only the sum of them. That is why all natural laws are based on numbers, and numbers are based on angles.

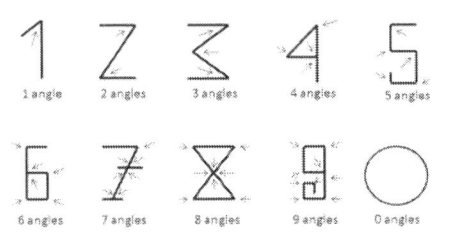

1 – 1 angle
2 – 2 angles
3 – 3 angles
4 – 4 angles
5 – 5 angles
6 – 6 angles
7 – 7 angles
8 – 8 angles
9 – 9 angles
0 – 0 angles

Therefore, space is based on geometry, and geometry is based on angles, and angles are based on extension, on all the potential extensions and their spreading out in eternity. Since angles are the foundation for numbers, arithmetic and geometry are therefore the same, only in different proportions.

Together with space, time occurs as well; expansion of the universe without intervals could not happen. The interval enables the expansion, and vice versa.

Both space and time occur in the same way the circle of the Absolute becomes the point or the 'divine particle'. Hence, space is limitless and unconditioned, as is time. Therefore, at the same time there is time and timelessness, the eternal present as well as the experience of existing during a specific period of time. This exists simultaneously, in the same way in which the Absolute exists simultaneously as its exact opposite - the point or 'the divine particle', a single one that generates a multitude of phenomena.

This is the way in which the Absolute is manifested as existence. In this way, everything is connected into One. This enables the results of quantum physics, which are seemingly contradictory (experiments with double slits, non-local communication, particles that exist in two places at the same time, etc.) - results which show that particles exist both as waves and as particles, depending on our point of observation. *If it were not so, if particles really existed both as entities and as a multitude, these results would not be possible. Subatomic particles would not exist in the form of waves and in the form of particles, nor would they have their ability of instant communication with one another no matter how far apart, irrelevant of space and time. This is possible only because everything that exists, all elements and objects, is the manifestation of the one and only 'divine particle,' which is independent from space and time and possesses all the qualities of the divine Absolute, which is at the same time everything and nothing.*

Owing to this fact, existence exists in the holographic form, where every particle reflects the whole.

For this reason, existence does not exist in time and space, but time and space exist in existence; this means that everything exists in parallel, all realities and all possibilities are already present. When living beings and objects move and change, they do not change really, for they do not exist substantially, as objects; it is just parallel realities replacing one another, where those which were hidden stepping out in the open to become visible.

In all of existence, nothing new happens, as everything which appears is only a transition from a state that lay dormant to one that is manifested.

The proofs keep piling up that there are speeds far larger than that of light, which mainstream science does not bring out in the open; *as well as our reality which we call matter and the physical world, that exists only because there are speeds much greater than the speed of light, enabled by the momentary movement of one 'divine particle'.*

We discover all of this with meditation because it represents a conscious return to the original state of the Absolute, and enables the act of knowing the unity of everything.

THE NATURE OF ENERGY

Energy is the vibration of the 'divine particle'. Energy is, by definition, existence or being in motion. Existence exists on the basis of vibrations of the one and only 'divine particle'. Its current vibrations give the energy for movement to all of existence. Therefore, all of existence is expressed in frequencies; all colours differ only with differing photon frequencies, all atoms of all elements differ only by the frequencies of their subatomic particles, which then differ only by the local frequency of the one and only 'divine particle' which constitutes everything. For this reason, all existence is energy, which is indestructible.

Frequencies adjust to their circumstances and needs. The whole Absolute vibrates to express all of its possibilities. That is why its frequencies are not the same everywhere and why they do not repeat themselves. The original state of energy is light. All of energy is life-giving energy. This is the connection between life and light.

Let us take a closer look at what energy actually is and how it occurs.

The 'divine particle' does not exist in the form of some physical particle, it is actually a fine vibration in the form of a torus.

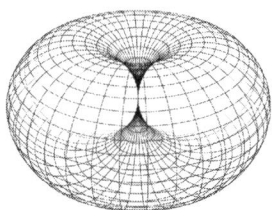

Everything in nature is only a vibration, and the basis for this vibration is the shape of the torus. The entire universe always vibrates in the shape of a torus. Galaxies, stars, planets, all living beings, all molecules and atoms, all electrons have the shape of a torus. The electron is just a coherent resonance in a toroidal field, not a particle; atoms are the same, as is everything with a more complex structure; everything is, in its most rudimentary form, just a resonant field without any materiality. Vibrations make toroidal fields, and toroidal fields in their movement create electromagnetism, together with electrical energy, all of which is based on the toroidal shape. In its rougher expression it is manifested as light, as sound and as magnetism, which exists all round us and in everything. This is known to us as ferromagnetism, which has iron, but there is a hidden fact as well: there exists paramagnetism and diamagnetism in all materials. They are weaker and different, but they create the dynamics of life in which we exist. They are everywhere, from life and electric energy to gravity. Magnetic fields are toroidal fields. There are no poles in them, as a torus is positive and negative on both sides, it is one field that functions in opposite directions, with centrifugal and centripetal forces which operate opposite to one another. Equatorial space is created between them in the shape of a disc. Every planet has this, even Earth, which is why all toroidal fields rotate in the shape of the disc, from the solar system to galaxies - which are also large toroidal fields. Even our bodies have a toroidal energy field.

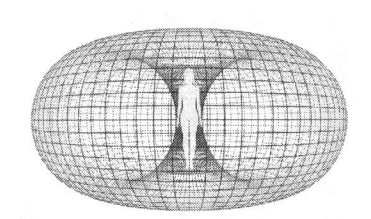

In the centre of each torus there is a 'zero point' or a small 'black hole' which is actually ether, or the Absolute itself. In this way, the Absolute vibrates in the form of the 'divine particle,' which again vibrates in the form of torus, and toroidal fields give off all the energy that exists, from life and electromagnetics to gravity.

Why does the Absolute vibrate in the shape of the torus in the first place? Because it vibrates within itself, as nothing is possible outside of it. A torus is the only possible shape for a circular movement of vibrations which is not completely closed and static, as a circle is, but it can also act in all possible ways, always remaining whole.

Due to the toroidal shape of the original vibration of the Absolute and 'divine particle', the universe exists as a hologram in which the original vibration of the 'divine particle' keeps being repeated, in all variants and in all possible ways. Interestingly enough, because of the torus shape, the Absolute always remains within while manifesting all relative phenomena. This is proven by the data based on measuring the background radiation (the Planck satellite, 2013), which proved that the universe is a hologram. When it is observed from Earth, it looks like the earth is in the centre of the cosmos. The measurements of the background radiation have shown conclusively that the entire universe exists according to the model of the torus, which, like the Earth, has an equatorial region in the middle of its sphere that's aligned with the Earth's ecliptic and equinox (which astrophysicists have named the 'Axis of Evil' - possibly because these results threaten to undermine all of their previous fabrications about the nature of reality, which they used as grounds to build their careers on), and that all background radiation is going in the direction of the Earth, from all sides. This acts as proof that we are in the centre of the cosmos, and that once again proves the key role of the observer, or the conscious subject. However, this is not proof that there is some centre and that we are in it. This is because the universe is a hologram, and every observer can see the same image of the cosmos as we see from Earth, from any angle of the cosmos. Because of the holographic nature of the universe, each point of observation is equal to all other points. For the holographic whole there is no up and down, left and right, centre and perimeter.

Meditation is the method which reveals that there is also no difference between the external and the internal. The fact that we are aware of the nature of the universe, even if only through the knowledge we have regarding background radiation, proves that consciousness in us goes beyond the manifested universe. Consciousness has to be above that which it tries to become aware of. This intrinsic, transcendental consciousness can only be strengthened with meditation.

In meditation, we become aware of the energy, and we realize that it is the functional expression of the consciousness of the divine Absolute. Meditation means the entire being is still. **When we sit with our legs crossed and our hands folded, completely relaxed and oblivious to the surrounding world, we close the energy of our being within the field of a torus - we take it back to its original energy field.** This conscious resting is nothing but the act of becoming aware of the essence of movement, becoming aware of the nature of existence as a vibration. Therefore, do not be deceived by the mind and its contradictions, because it often shows things to be the opposite of what they truly are. Calmness in meditation is not a negation of movement, but the final goal of all the movement of the cosmos, the highest form of awareness of all movement and action, and awareness of existence as a vibration of consciousness, as divine energy. When we become one with the divine movement that manifests itself, then movement disappears, and only the divine is left; and then we are calm and peaceful, we have found ourselves in the divine Absolute, with its every movement. To be more accurate, with meditative resting we cross over from the illusion of individual existence, in which there is only the illusion of movement, to that in which all movements are, the ultimate, widest whole of all occurrence - and that is the realm of the Absolute. Movement disappears, together with space and time, and then we become aware that only the divine Absolute exists as itself, because nothing outside of it is even possible. It is every movement and all energy. Everything is moving towards some outcome. In meditation, this outcome is discovered within ourselves. Meditation is tranquility. In such meditation, the difference between movement and stillness disappears, together with the disappearance of the illusion of separation between all phenomena and the divine Absolute itself. Then, meditation itself finally disappears, because it also exists in existence. However, in order to reach this level of consciousness, our first task is to overcome movement with tranquility. Meditation is the act of empowering the consciousness, which goes beyond all of the manifested universe, until we realize that that consciousness is the manifested universe. Then we finally come to know ourselves in such a way that we realize we were the only factor separating our consciousness and the manifested universe from the Absolute; there cannot be a 'we' because there is no duality, there is nothing but the Absolute. When there is nothing else, then there really is nothing, ourselves included. Only then is our view on reality is clean and clear, cleansed from all uncertainties which only exist in the eye of the beholder. When the observer is so pure that there is nothing between the observer and the observed, then the observed can be seen as energy, and energy as consciousness; it can be seen that the observed is no different from the observer; that everything is merely consciousness of oneself.

THE NATURE OF CONSCIOUSNESS

We have seen that the basic frequency of existence is based on the primary projection of the Absolute into its utmost opposite point, or the 'divine particle', which vibrates much faster than the speed of light, literally instantly, thus shaping everything in space and time, in the entire universe. The transformation of the Absolute into its opposite point is the basic contradiction from which all contradictions in nature occur, and all polarities too. That original contradiction enables the vibration of the 'divine particle' from which everything that exists originates. It is based on polarities. The core of everything is electromagnetism, which is also based on polarity. The original polarity of the Absolute and the point is reflected in all existing life as the energetic polarity which is defined by a zero and one, as information. In this way, vibration at the same time becomes information. Information is at the base of all vibrations, and all vibrations of the cosmos are in their essence one global information field.

All information exists because of the one who becomes aware of it. Without awareness it would not exist. They are basically one, but they are expressed as separate, as space and time. When space and time are compressed and disappear, then the information has arrived to the conscious subject, and became consciousness. The supreme subject of awareness of everything is the divine Absolute. Therefore, everything originates from it and everything disappears into it. In the same way that the Absolute is projected into a multitude of phenomena by means of its opposition, the 'divine particle', all information is also projected because of the one who is aware of it. Those are not two different things: the Absolute who is projected in multiple vibrations which is information, and the awareness of information in a conscious subject, boil down to one and the same thing. The conscious subject is the reason and the goal of expressing all information, all vibrations of the cosmos, all shapes of cosmic events.

This is also indicated in the cosmological theory of the Strong Anthropic Principle (SAP), according to which all visible features of the universe are not the product of coincidence or natural selection, but are the consequence of a special purpose: creating the conditions for the occurrence of the conscious subject. This principle says: 'the universe must have such properties which allows for the development of life in some stadium of its existence'. The logical conclusion is that the universe was created with the purpose of occurrence and survival of the observer, and the observers in question are necessary for the existence of the universe (Final Anthropic Principle (FAP)).

Not only does the Strong Anthropic Principle say that nature exists exactly in the form it does, but that it cannot exist any differently in order to be able to create a conscious subject. Nature cannot be without a conscious subject. *He is primary. He induces the origin of nature.*

The large-scale conscious subject is the Absolute, and its small-scale version is the human. They are basically the same, because nothing is possible in the divine Absolute that is beyond itself.

In this way, existence is not different from consciousness, and consciousness is not different from existence. Everything exists, all the vibrations that are comprised of all the energy and all the information, due to the existence of the conscious subject, who is basically the divine Absolute itself; and we are it, to the extent to which we can understand all this.

The basic information follows the simplicity of the Absolute's manifestation, from the abstract and comprehensive circle to its opposition, the point. That universal contradiction is manifested as information in the form of one and zero (1 and 0), and plus and minus, (+ and -) of electromagnetic polarity. All life energy is expressed according to the principle of polarity of the male and female sex; all physical energy lies in the electromagnetic force in the form of + and -; and all information technology in 1 and 0. Therefore, electromagnetism is at the base of all natural processes, from the subatomic to the cosmic. Hence, electromagnetism is essentially the information process, and that is why all of life is actually a conscious process. There is no life without consciousness. Life energy is basically an information process, because energy is a vibration, and every vibration is information. Life exists because of awareness, because of perception. Consciousness is at the base of all manifestation and development of nature. All the cells of our body are alive and they can be alive only because they are currently communicating with all the other cells of our body; they represent a symbiotic whole. Their communication is not only instantaneous with every other cell in our body, but with all of nature as well. Life relies on that conscious whole. Life is consciousness - the consciousness of the Absolute of itself.

At the base of everything, there is a conscious intention of the Absolute to manifest itself in all shapes, including all physical things which you can see right before your eyes, this book which you are reading now (yes, especially the book), and every possible experience and phenomenon. The Earth you walk on is the divine consciousness which supports you and provides ground to live on; the air you breath is the divine breath that gives you life; the rock on the side of the road is the divine consciousness which chose to be that rock. The thoughts that you have in your head are not your thoughts at all, but information of the divine of itself, as well as of all its peculiarities and possibilities. All the events you experience are movements and actions of the divine consciousness, which guide you in the drama of experiencing all the possibilities of existence, in an attempt to understand the meaning of everything that is happening.

Awareness of and the ability to understand the divine has been called 'seeing God face to face' by mystics; wherever they look, they see God. They always look at Him and touch Him, He is everything and everywhere, and that is why they always feel veneration and bliss toward everything; they respect equally all events and objects and beings, they always have inner peace and tranquility in the divine presence, that nothing from the outside world can upset or perturb.

Meditation is a process of systematic awareness which never happens in nature or in existence spontaneously or of its own accord. Only in the consciousness of the Absolute can a similar awareness of itself happen in the way it happens in deep meditation, in samadhi. The man in meditation, therefore, repeats the essential awareness of the Absolute according to which everything exists; he makes his way back to the original divine consciousness. Since he can never be outside of it, because it is everything that is, the returning is experienced only as a revival and awakening.

CONSCIOUSNESS AND ENERGY REFLECT THE NATURE OF THE ABSOLUTE

The primordial act of the Absolute turning itself into its opposition point, or 'the divine particle' and continuing to do so every single moment, enables the creation of all reality and the manifestation of itself in everything. The energy lies in that basic polarity; it gives movement to all of existence, which we experience as energy and life.

Consciousness also lies in the same contradiction, but here it is necessary to explain the nature of consciousness a little better. Consciousness is the very divine Absolute; it is the only source of consciousness that occurs in all shapes of existence. However, the Absolute vibrates in every moment into its contradiction, the 'divine particle' and in such a way that *every moment consists of the manifestation of the Absolute and its returning back to its unmanifested state.* In this way, the nature of the Absolute always remains the same, otherwise it would not be absolute; every manifested existence is no different from the Absolute; the source of consciousness, the Absolute, is never separated from all of manifested existence, and consciousness is always at the base of all existence, present in everything without any transference. It is fundamentally no different from existence; in this way consciousness is expressed in existence through the dialectics of the opposite of the manifested and unmanifested Absolute; *it springs up between two moments which consist of the manifested state and the return to the unmanifested state of the Absolute*. Although it springs up between two moments of primordial contradiction of existence, those contradictions, to a higher or a lower degree, have an influence on the presence of consciousness. For this reason it is inherent in the nature of consciousness to participate in a game of opposites, to its ultimate ability, but also to be the basis for overcoming all contradictions, to transcend existence. Consequently, consciousness is neutral, independent of all states of existence; it is never imposed, it can easily be suppressed by rougher vibrations, it remains strong only to reveal its absolute nature, it always waits to be revealed and it can do so only in the appeasement of all discrepancies in human being. Consciousness cannot be strengthened because it is always authentic, it is always the same, in everything; its presence is strengthened by removing the contradictions of inauthentic existence which keep it in the dark.

    Meditation consists entirely of establishing and strengthening this original consciousness, through the discipline of removing all opposites of manifested existence in the area of microcosm, the human body. Meditation does not strengthen consciousness, but only calms the body and mind so that consciousness can be expressed more strongly. Thus, through the man in meditation, the strengthening of the presence of the divine Absolute in this relative world can occur.

    Because of all this, consciousness can also be understood as perception. Consciousness is the basis of existence for the same reason that the divine Absolute has expressed itself as its exact opposite, as a single point, and by doing so set in motion all of manifestation, namely existence: for the sake of self-knowledge, and to experience all of its possibilities, because all of existence expresses all of the possibilities of the divine Absolute. Everything-that-is was expressed and exists now as everything-that-can-be. Therefore, the reason for existence is in perception; the basis of consciousness is the Absolute perceiving all of its possibilities, which are manifested throughout existence, from subatomic energy in the form of the information field, to the perception of all living beings. The divine Absolute recognizes itself through perception of all living beings, through all of existence. In this way, consciousness and existence are one, and that one is the divine Absolute. Nothing else exists but this.

Since the source of consciousness is the Absolute itself, the consciousness that we use every day is only a tiny reflection of the same consciousness of the Absolute, the consciousness which enables all of existence. For that reason, we can detect every type of existence using our consciousness. Consciousness is the same everywhere, there is no multitude of consciousnesses, as there is no multitude of Absolutes or multitude of existences.

THE DIMENSIONS OF EXISTENCE

Existence expands from the finest quantum field to the rough forms of the physical world that we can see in space and time. The principle of simplicity is present here, as well; vibrations keep expanding from their most subtle form to their roughest equivalent.

Esoteric knowledge has symbolically represented this most subtle dimension of existence, the information field of nature, with the element of air.

The information field is expressed as the energy of life, and its symbolic representation is the element of fire.

When they come together, information and energy must create some form; however, this is not necessarily a concrete physical shape, but rather a fluid form that prepares itself, in a number of ways, to materialize. This is the world of astral, which is symbolically represented with the element of water.

When all these elements and dimensions are joined together, the concrete physical element is made, which is both symbolically and realistically represented as the element of earth.

This is the four-pole principle of the creation of everything, starting from the finest vibration, information and energy, to concrete realization.

In esoteric science it is known as tetragrammaton, the name of God, JHVH.

While they are in the highest dimension, air, all possibilities of existence are compressed in a timeless one, in the implicit information order of the quantum field; as they begin to descend into lower dimensions, the shapes (information) become more and more explicit, more rough and more concrete in space and time. The pyramidal scheme is as follows:

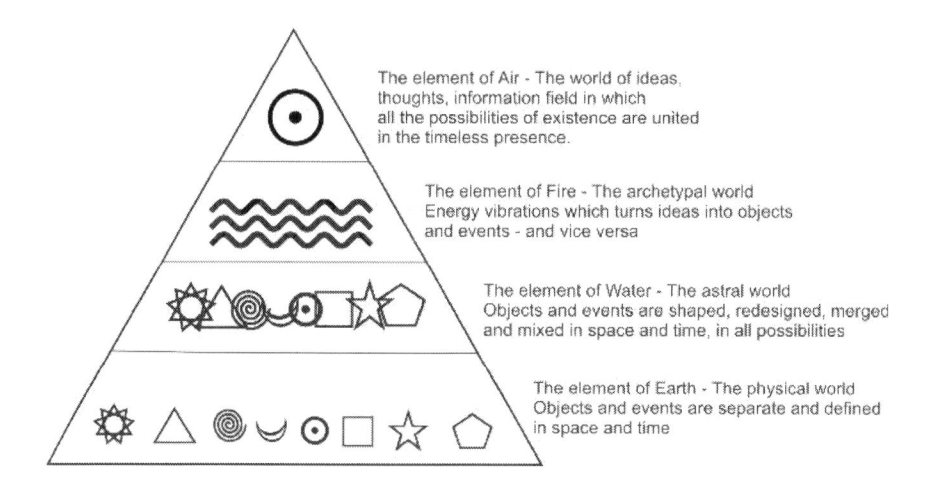

The element of Air - The world of ideas, thoughts, information field in which all the possibilities of existence are united in the timeless presence.

The element of Fire - The archetypal world Energy vibrations which turns ideas into objects and events - and vice versa

The element of Water - The astral world Objects and events are shaped, redesigned, merged and mixed in space and time, in all possibilities

The element of Earth - The physical world Objects and events are separate and defined in space and time

The pyramid structure of the manifestations of all of the dimensions of existence in reality represents the change of frequencies, from the finest original one which has non-Hertzian properties of timeless integrity, to the roughest Hertzian frequency with its properties of three-dimensional reality. The top of the pyramid is a non-Hertzian timeless presence, and its base is the Hertzian separation of objects.

In our experience, this pyramid structure shows that everything is one, but we see that unity differently, depending on what dimensions we observe from, and what state of mind we're in. Each of these dimensions represents a specific state of consciousness in man. Only on the physical plane do all objects, phenomena and events look as though they're separate from one another. Only there does man experience alienation to the fullest, only there do all events that the conscious mind experiences as reality seem separate - only while in the physical body. However, on the astral plane, objects, phenomena and events can mix in ways which are not possible in the physical world; they can even be recreated at will. In higher dimensions, everything becomes more and more united into One. Everything is One, in fact, it is only expressed as a multitude of possibilities so that people can experience temptation and awareness. Objects and events, on the physical plane, may seem separate and without obvious connection because we cannot see their meaning; but if we were to rise to the higher dimensions we would realize the connectedness of everything into one meaningful whole. Only in the physical can we see the fragments and apparent separation of all objects and events, only here do we live in the illusion of alienation; and then we ask questions like: 'Why does God allow evil?'. If we were to rise to the higher dimensions, which becomes easy once we master the consciousness of those dimensions, the potential for which already exists in us, and if we see things from the highest dimension, from the element of air, where space and time are completely united and have disappeared, we would see that there is no world outside of ourselves, that we are the conscious subject of the objective world, that everything is the perfect Whole, the Absolute, that is at the same time our essence, the Self. Everything is a reflection of the Whole, of our Self, and for that reason everything is perfect; the universe could not exist if there were flaws in it.

As the prism disperses one beam of light into all the colours of the rainbow, the same principle follows the pyramid structure: the frequencies of reality reflect one reality into various dimensions and a multitude of possibilities of existence.

In the context of the dimensions of existence, meditation should be understood as a method of ascending into all the higher dimensions, from the rough world of isolated objects in the space and time continuum, toward a finer field in which space and time are compressed into One, into an awareness of itself. ***In the man who meditates, space and time of all the existence are compressed into their final outcome.***

Above this pyramid structure of all the dimensions of existence there is ether or *akasha*, a term used in old books; the modern name is the universal quantum field. All the potentials of existence reside in it, grouped together into the timeless One. Everything gets expressed in space and time from this field, and in this way there is nothing new; everything that appears in existence has already existed in the universal quantum field, or ether. Only the manifestation of an already existing phenomena can happen, never the creation of something new, something which has never existed before. In this way, the existence exists in two ways: unmanifested and manifested. Our physical, sensory observation is only familiar with the manifested aspect. Unmanifested and manifested phenomena exist side by side, simultaneously, or to be more precise, timelessly. They possess the characteristic of being the timeless manifestation of the Absolute into its opposition, the 'divine particle'.

The ether or *akasha* is the source and the basis of all manifestation, and because of it all of existence in all its dimensions has a pyramid structure; that is, condensed in space and time. The pyramid structure clearly depicts how this simultaneous existence of the multitude of beings in time (the basis of pyramid, the element of earth) and the unison of everything in the timeless presence (the top of the pyramid, the element of air) is possible.

Everything is essentially one timeless presence. For that reason, there is no process during which one transforms into the other, because all dimensions exist simultaneously, all are manifested, and they keep manifesting every single moment; their distinction happens only in man's mind, during the time he resides in the lowest and slowest dimension.

There is no difference in the divine consciousness which is in the element of air and in the element of earth, because it is manifested in all elements at the same time. All the differences exist only in the mind of the observer, in man during the process of his identification with the body, which is only in one dimension, the physical, the most limited dimension. The more man manages to surpass his identification with the body and mind, the more he gets to know the higher dimensions, up to the point when he recognizes the identical presence of the divine consciousness in all dimensions at the same time. In other words: the universal quantum field contains within itself all that exists, both manifested and unmanifested states. The old name for ether or the quantum field is *akasha*, and in Sanskrit this means space. Therefore, the quantum field is not some micro world only physicists can reach, nor some abstract higher dimension - we are always in the quantum field, in the space where existence happens. Everything that we can see before our eyes is that field, everything is comprised of it, everything we touch and everything we have within and without. It is the most supreme divine reality.

Meditation is a systematic method with which we enable our consciousness to become open to that possibility, which is already here and now.

With meditation we are not rising from one reality to another, that's somehow higher or better, because all we can actually do is to get to know this one better. When we become aware of what it truly is, then we can see nothing but the most supreme divine reality. As a direct consequence, reality itself suddenly becomes divine, and it can no longer be destructive. It acted that way only because it was part divine mind, and part human. It reflected the state of consciousness of the conscious subject, to whom it served as a mirror. It was destructive exactly to the point of man's alienation from the divine consciousness. It has, like a mirror, reflected that illusory separation. In the unity between the individual human mind and the absolute divine consciousness, nothing can ever be destructive.

The outer physical world and life will become perfect only when man becomes aware of them, in all dimensions, when the divine consciousness realizes itself in all aspects and possibilities through the man who has reached this highest level of awareness.

Meditation is a way in which people grow in systematic awareness of all dimensions.

MAN IS A MICROCOSM

All of the dimensions of existence progressively construct both the cosmos and all beings. While in nature they are manifested with more or less participation, trying out all of the possibilities and combinations, at the end of the day they merge into one being that possesses a full perception of existence - not only to observe, but also to understand the meaning of what's observed. That being is man.

Man is the final act in the manifestation of the cosmos. He is the cosmos in miniature, or as a microcosm.

Man has the ability to think - which belongs in the element of air. Thinking is the ability to summarize information independently of space and time; our thoughts enable us to make sense of everything we encounter in space and time, the past as well as the present and future, in all their aspects and possibilities.

Man, with his ideas and thoughts, directs the energy of achievement, intention and will. This is the element of fire.

Man gives shape to his imagination, in the astral, in reality and in his sleep; he gives shape to the objects and ideas he has imagined and intends to accomplish. This is the element of water.

Man realizes the ideas and intentions he has imagined through a concrete action on the physical plane: the element of earth.

All of the dimensions of nature are the inner dimensions of man. Man consists of all the dimensions in nature. Therefore man, being allowed such a high degree of freedom in his consciousness, may leave his body and linger in the higher dimensions, where he discovers his own inner, unconscious world. Such experiences of higher dimensions are experienced spontaneously, whilst people are dreaming and sleeping, but they experience them as their unconscious contents. This is because man is not truly aware of his real nature, of the fact that all the dimensions of nature are his inner states. Everything is in him. Man is unconscious only because he searches for something outside himself.

All of the states of consciousness and all of the shapes of existence exist in parallel, because nothing is substantial and everything is a hologram made up of one single 'divine particle'. However, man can become aware of his true nature, and then, according to the words of Advaita Vedanta, see everything in himself and himself in everything; or by the testimonies of Gnostic devotees: 'As above, so below, nothing is outward or inward only'. You see God (the Kingdom Come) in yourself and all round.

Upon leaving his body man enters his higher dimensions, which already co-exist in parallel. Therefore it is not entirely correct to say that he leaves his body; essentially there is nothing to leave because everything is One. All of existence is in the body of man. He only passes from one parallel reality into another, passing from one state of consciousness into another. This is why existence can be the subject of man's consciousness, in order for him to discover its meaning. Man reaches the meaning of life through the drama of temptation and all the possibilities of existence, through karma and destiny. Through man, the divine Absolute comes to full awareness of itself, to the meaning of all manifestation and existence. God recognizes himself through man. Man recognizes God through himself. This is the same act.

We will better understand what all of this means when we present one more fact. We have said that the 'divine particle' currently vibrates in all possible ways, and in that manner expresses all the possibilities of manifestation of the divine Absolute, because existence is awareness of the divine of itself. All these vibrations are momentary, and every moment consists of a complete resetting of the 'divine particle' to its initial state, to the state of the unmanifested Absolute. In other words, **the divine Absolute is manifested, every moment, in the form of the overall existence, and every moment it returns to itself, into an unmanifested state.** In this way, existence is inseparable from the Absolute. All of this is possible because the essence of existence is beyond space and time. Because of the constant returning and dissolving of the Absolute into itself, in between every two moments in the existence of everything, the consciousness of the Absolute is always available to all of existence. It does not need to travel anywhere. It is here, together with every moment, with every vibration of the 'divine particle'. This is the way in which consciousness and existence are one.

Now, *since man is a microcosm*, which means he is the embodiment of all the possibilities of perception of existence, and he holds the ability to recognize the meaning of manifestation in general, meaning the Absolute, hence: *man, in his existence, reflects the existence of the Absolute. Man, as the microcosm, constantly resets from a manifested existence into his unmanifested state. The two phases, the change from one to the other in man's experience, correspond to when man is in his awakened state, and in a state of deep dreamless sleep*. These states correspond with the transformation of the unmanifested Absolute into its exact opposite state, the 'divine particle' or manifested existence, and the return to an unmanifested state of the Absolute. ***Deep sleep in man is the analogue of the unmanifested Absolute, and the materialistic reality found in the awakened state is the analogue of the manifestation of the Absolute in the form of a multitude of phenomena and the entire manifested cosmos.*** Everything that happens on a global scale also happens on a small scale, in man, because the universe is a hologram. To say that the universe is a hologram means that in the entire manifestation of the universe, nothing happens but a primordial manifestation of the Absolute into its opposition point, or one 'divine particle'. This one and only manifestation, this single moment, keeps repeating itself, in all possible versions according to the model of the 'golden cross-section,' which, with its increasing complexity, creates all the possible shapes of existence. This is why in all the shapes of existence the 'golden cross-section' can be seen, because the Absolute is reflected in everything.

Through man the Absolute repeats itself and becomes self-aware, in all possible ways; in addition, it attains a sense of itself, of its manifestation. Becoming aware is the ultimate goal of the manifestation of the world, the ultimate goal and purpose of existence. It is realized through man. Man achieves this when he consciously comes to his initial, authentic state, which he is able to reach in deep dreamless sleep. This is the state of samadhi, or deep meditation, in which consciousness is completely recognized as existence and existence as consciousness - and all of it together as man's essence, soul or Self.

The purpose of meditation is to make conscious everything which happens spontaneously in man. Then, when the meditant achieves a state of being where he is always conscious and awakened, both in his awakened state and in deep sleep, then he becomes equal to the Absolute which is ever-present in everything, both as the manifested and the unmanifested. Existence always exists, in the same way that consciousness in man should always exist, because it is always one with the existence. When man reaches this state, he is enlightened.

Then, for that man, space of the manifested world disappears, because he cannot distinguish it from himself any more. Time, in which reality is not what it actually is, also disappears. ***Time and space exist only as an illusion that shows reality as something else, and not the timeless Absolute, here and now.*** Then, according to the words of Nagarjuna, the shape ('divine particle') becomes the emptiness (Absolute), and the emptiness becomes the shape, samsara and nirvana are one. The purpose of all this is for everything which happens, unconsciously and spontaneously, to become conscious. Only man can realize this through himself, realize it with his own will and understanding, by becoming aware of himself. The state of unison with existence which he spontaneously and unconsciously experiences in deep dreamless sleep should be achieved consciously during meditation. Therefore, by becoming aware of himself, man becomes aware of the world; by perfecting himself, he perfects the world. It is not possible any other way, because man is the microcosm, the holographic reflection of the cosmos.

In a man who meditates, in samadhi, the unity of consciousness and existence finds its completion and realizes the purpose of the manifestation of the universe. Hence the inner peace found in samadhi: the manifestation of the Absolute has reached its ultimate purpose and has overcome the motion of the universe. The entire universe is intent on moving towards itself, within itself, because in the holographic universe there is nothing outside of itself.

In the man who has become aware of himself through meditation, in samadhi, the awareness of the Absolute of itself is the most complete and the most perfect manifestation of itself.

All other manifestations are the expression of some degree of unbalance and incompleteness. The entire manifested universe is the expression of imbalance of consciousness in the game of contradictions. That is why the entire universe disappears in meditation. That is why man begins to exist in reality only at that moment.

WE EXPERIENCE OUR TIMELESSNESS THROUGH TIME

The definition of the origin of space is that space is the current transformation of the Absolute into its opposite, the 'divine particle'. It also provides us with the definition of time, because for each spatial shaping an interval is needed.

We have stated that the 'divine particle' itself is timeless, like the Absolute, and that it currently manifests itself into all its possibilities; however, even though reality is essentially timeless, it is practically impossible for various complex and rough shapes, which are made from one particle, to exist simultaneously in one place. They are manifested, in their roughest form, in a three-dimensional physical shape; they undergo metamorphosis with every interval that constitutes time. In accordance with the dimensions, they manifest every rough three-dimensional shape (the element of earth), which is just information in the highest dimension (the element of air). That information in man is an idea or a thought. The information of all shapes cannot exist simultaneously, they change consecutively because of observation. The linear track of information or thought creates the illusion of time. One thought occurs before another; in the same way, one shape appears to be closer to the observer, and another seems farther away.

Therefore, the definition of time is possible only as a mental or 'spiritual' experience of intervals in which the Absolute looks like it is not what it actually is in every moment. That is why it is inaccurate to speak about space and time as separate categories; they are one, so we speak of space-time.

Since nothing is outside the Absolute, not even ourselves, for us time is a state during which it mentally appears to us that we are not what we (in absolute terms) really are.

Since time exists only as an illusion that reality is something else and not the timeless Absolute that it is, this illusion is our destiny and karma. Time is the space for the events of destiny and karma; it is a period in which we are under the illusion that the highest reality is something else, not what it really is (a timeless existence of every single moment, here and now). This is why our life in time is like a dream, an illusion, ignorance of existence, maya. Also, time exists as a means of self-realization. We need time to realize what we've done and why, to re-examine and correct the mistakes, and to strengthen our consciousness. We further need time to mature and do what is needed in the space where we live, and to become aware of the production processes of every job and all events, to find the meaning in everything. In order to become aware of the meaning of events, we have to become aware of the nature of consciousness; with the awareness of consciousness we become truly aware of existence itself, because in the final outcome they are one and the same. In other words, consciousness is all-that-is, the Absolute, and it is manifested as everything-that-can-be, as all events.

Man's destiny and karma are manifested in space and time as material culture and civilization, all the work and creativity of man in this world. Man's destiny and karma shape the outer space, the world in which he lives. And all of it exists so he can make sense of everything. Becoming aware of meaning happens as a result of the compression of time in the present moment.

Within man, time and space are compressed to generate karmic maturity and self-awareness. The time-space of our existence is a state in which we are not what we truly are. Therefore, the chief characteristic of our existence is the constant search for ourselves, our essence and soul, while in the set conditions of the outer world we seek love and understanding from others. Typically, we are on the constant lookout for soul mates, and at the same time we are trying to find the perfect spot for living comfortably. All of our states in space-time boil down to the search of awareness of ourselves; we keep building our civilization as a consequence of our aspirations towards understanding the existence and ourselves, through the experience of creating exterior shapes, and all our culture is a direct consequence of our aspirations towards mutual understanding between people and the understanding of existence. All our interpersonal relationships add up to an enhanced awareness of ourselves; our psychodynamics lead to understanding ourselves. In this way, we, being lost in time, shape ourselves and our living space. All our lives, all incarnations in space and time have one common denominator: an ongoing quest for self-awareness.

Our souls are embodied to be able to express consciousness of their divine essence despite such horrid conditions and limitations in the body.

When man's self-awareness equals God-awareness, and such the experience of consciousness of the soul occurs, time and space are dissolved into the timeless present, which to the awakened man appears in the form of the divine presence. The disappearance of space and time is nothing but an awareness of consciousness, knowledge that there is nothing outside the divine Absolute, that everything is only us playing the game according to our rules.

The space-time of our existence can best be compressed in meditation. Meditation is physical stillness, the discontinuation of movement in space and the cessation of any action. Meditation is mental calmness that causes time to stop. The end of wandering through space-time is possible only as an awakening in full awareness of oneself, one's own absolute essence or soul. There is no form of meditative calmness other than this; relaxation during the realization of our own outcome, the outcome of existence, which all of our lives have been moving in the direction of, and to which all life strives. Everything else is a stiffness which is imposed upon us and which counteracts life.

In the true meditative state 'Kingdom Come' is present on earth, like it is in heaven. It can find its presence only in man using his consciousness and actions. Such a man is the scientist of the future; he manifests the unity of consciousness and existence, he connects existence with meaning. This is the real essence of technology and science in general. Patanjali described such scientists in the Yoga Sutras, at the dawn of civilization in this world, as a scientifically defined unity of consciousness and existence in a man who meditates in samadhi. In more recent years, such a scientist who connected himself to the unity of consciousness and existence was Nikola Tesla. He showed with his own life and work that the only true science is natural science, the one that connects consciousness and existence, and which awakens existence; that is why he alerted us to the fact that all energy is already present. Tesla's work was only a reflection of his being and mind, and as such, they were exclusively in the service of existence and consciousness. Such must be the scientist of the future, or there will be no future. The man who connects consciousness and existence through himself and his work is the only true scientist of the future. Only can such a connection be real science. Without that connection, man only creates destruction.

At the very beginning of civilization, Patanjali showed man how to connect consciousness and existence in himself, through samadhi in self-awareness, in the science of yoga and meditation. The ultimate realization of the true meaning of science, civilization and material culture in this world will only be possible as an outer realization of the unity of consciousness and existence in man. Then and only then will the realization of man's essence, the soul, become reality, and with it the realization of the divine consciousness in this world.

THE EFFECT OF MEDITATION AND THE STRUCTURE OF HUMAN BEINGS

THE RELATIONSHIP BETWEEN MIND AND CONSCIOUSNESS OF THE SOUL

We have seen that the human being surpasses the physical body. The body is the lowest sanctuary of consciousness of the soul. Consciousness of our soul comes from the divine consciousness which enables everything and which is everything. From consciousness of our soul comes consciousness of our mind also, equipped with countless limitations. That is why consciousness of the mind is always connected with a level of understanding of the nature of reality. In order to understand the nature of reality, we firstly need to understand the nature of our being, the way it is organized. The simplest display of the organization of our being which everybody can recognize from their own experience is a division into the lower mind, the higher mind, and consciousness of the soul.

The basic structure of the divine consciousness which enables everything in human beings is:

1. ***Consciousness of the soul*** (which is transcendental and only partially embodied)

2. ***Higher mind*** (or higher I, which stands between the physical body and the divine consciousness of the soul, as the link between the two)

3. ***Consciousness of the physical mind*** (or ego, placed in the brain of the physical body).

HIGHER MIND

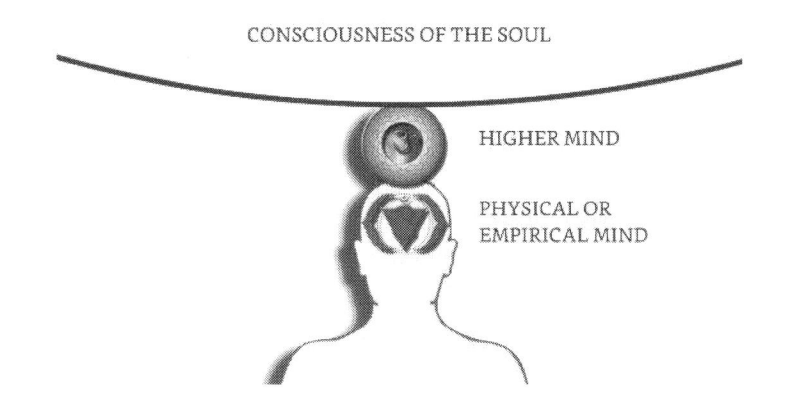

PHYSICAL OR EMPIRICAL MIND

Consciousness of the soul is massive - of such proportions that it cannot and should not fit into the physical body. So only a small part of consciousness of the soul is incarnated in the body, just enough for life. The body has a degree of consciousness, albeit elementary, and it's the one that manages the metabolism and the autonomic nervous system. Often there is a discrepancy between consciousness of the soul and the body, because not every body is ideal for consciousness of the soul that is currently incarnated in it. There is often the need for adjustment, which sometimes does not succeed completely. These are the cases of people who, for example, have an unstable life or are in conflict with themselves this conflict which is often described as the conflict between the 'lower' and the 'higher' nature in man, instinct and spirit, morality and immorality, good and evil.

Consciousness of the incarnated soul is determined by the level of karmic maturity and plans for its prospective life, including issues that may help raise awareness. The consciousness, character and temperament of the body are determined by a wider context, its background, including time and space of the birth of the body. This is best depicted in the science of astrology, because the universe is a hologram. Genetics, culture and climate also play an important part. Climate can have a big impact on temperament and character. Consciousness of the soul is always the same, but consciousness of the body grows at the same pace as a body grows, and gets stronger as it gathers impressions of life. In this way, consciousness of the body suppresses consciousness of the soul over time, which gets weaker and weaker gradually. Consciousness of the soul in a child is strong because the body is weak and untarnished by impressions, but it does not know how to express itself other than through simple and direct reactions, which quite often amaze adults. Children often see and foresee things grown people cannot. The power of the presence of the soul in the weak body of a child can be felt by adults, for it is that spirituality which comes from us and which we are able to express spontaneously in our communication with children; the unconditional love, nobility, responsibility and spirituality which adults spontaneously acquire only because they are in contact and in a relationship with children. People who treat children badly are 'soulless'; that is, consciousness of the soul in them is highly suppressed, to such measure that it cannot be expressed. The extent of suppression of consciousness of the soul is a measurement of the evil and misunderstanding they are capable of. The manifestation of consciousness of the soul is a measurement of goodness and understanding.

  The relationship between consciousness of the soul and consciousness of the body/mind changes and varies over time, over years, but sometimes on a daily basis as well. The dialectic is always unique and constitutes what is called 'personality'. The variations in their relationships instigates all the psychodrama a human being experiences in this world.

It is important to understand that it is not the goal of the consciousness of the soul to incarnate into the body unchanged and then to function smoothly in this world. If it were, nothing new would happen; there would be no new experiences to further crystallize consciousness of the soul. Likewise, it is not the purpose of consciousness of the body to act completely independently, because it cannot; if it did it would be an animal. The final purpose is the connection between consciousness of the soul and the body, which is what happens eventually. Therefore, there is nothing wrong or unnatural in consciousness of the soul being suppressed by the body over time; this gives consciousness of the soul the necessary oblivion and the chance to reach itself in the state of maximum suppression, to understand the opposing sides the divine consciousness aims to express, and to come to a point of understanding existence itself.

It is therefore important to understand that because of the strong pull of consciousness of the soul, we forget why we have come into this world; it is important to never feel repulsion towards anything, especially towards the body and material life. The purpose of the whole game is to acquire understanding through experience, preferably without conflicts and denial. The goal is to understand everything, not have victory over anything. However, it is the nature of the mind to function in opposites only, so it keeps imposing contradicting views on things, as if it were an issue of conflict between the soul and the body. This is why the conflict that exists between the soul and the body occurs - because of unbalanced activity in the mind. The soul only aspires toward understanding and to harmonize opposites; it always surpasses opposites, and this is known to us as awareness.

Consciousness of the soul comes for that reason only: to experience all opposites and all potentials of existence. Through the constant suppression and awareness of consciousness of the soul, the personality of man gets crystallized, and this personality connects all the opposites and in doing so it creates them, leading to understanding. Only the correct understanding of all opposites can return us to the divine through consciousness of the soul. This is the goal of incarnation of souls: to ensure an understanding of existence that will be suitable for the divine consciousness; to chew the existence in such a way that the divine is able to swallow. The divine consciousness already exists as existence itself, as nature, but completely impersonally. The purpose is for the divine consciousness of existence to express all of its abundant potential in man so that he learns to express himself personally, and with full understanding of himself, in all possible detail, and all potential opposites. The understanding of all opposites means the understanding of all possibilities. The individual who has a full understanding of opposites is complete personality. The understanding of all possibilities is the peak of creativity. A complete personality always expresses itself creatively; not necessarily in a monumental and grand way, but through numerous tiny details that enrich life. In this way, the complete personality of a human being is the highest pinnacle of creativity of the divine creation; that is, of manifestation. The divine has nothing more to do. This is the point of the return of the divine consciousness to itself. It is the beginning of meditation.

The small part of consciousness of soul which is incarnated is not directly present in the physical body, but it has a mediator (the higher mind), which also isn't in the body but a little above it, in the higher, astral plane. **The** *higher mind and consciousness of the soul are able to make an impact on the body with proximity only, in the role of witnesses.* The higher mind has to be independent from the body in order to be a good mediator for consciousness of the soul; it must not be disturbed by the body. However, it must be close enough to be able to establish a constant connection between the body and the mind.

The higher mind influences the lower mind by providing it with a higher and wider perspective; it sees from the higher dimension everything that happens in a wider context, independently from time and space, and that is why it can give information to the lower, physical mind or ego, which generally has a very limited perspective and can see only what is observable by the senses. Information from the higher mind comes to the physical mind as inspiration or intuition, a sudden insight in everyday living, but also through dreams, when the physical mind is suppressed and the higher mind can act more easily. These pieces of information can also be independent from space and time, and this is why they can appear in the form of clairvoyance as well.

All religious and mystical experiences are a reflection of connecting the physical or empirical mind with consciousness of the soul through the higher mind. Sometimes, this connection is wrongly interpreted as 'conversations with God' or a 'guardian angel'. In short, all objective knowledge in this world has come from the higher mind, which forwards consciousness of the soul into the body and the lower mind. All discipline and culture in this world is an attempt to train the lower mind to be open and fit for the insights which come from the higher mind. Although it has to be said that there are also cultures which function differently, which make it their aim to prevent merging with the higher consciousness.

They serve the purpose of the dialectic of direct opposites which crystallizes consciousness of the soul.

Practically, insight from the higher mind acts so that if, for example, we meet a person who has committed a crime but has managed to evade justice, we know instinctively upon him that something is wrong, that he is hiding something. Children can feel this immediately. Although our rational, physical mind cannot see anything and is not in possession of any information regarding the history of that individual, the higher mind will send warning signals which the lower mind understands as intuition or a 'hunch' and which indicates that there is some other truth than the one being physically shown. We will feel emotional discomfort towards that person. Hence the proverb 'God knows everything'; this is an indirect way of saying that consciousness of the higher mind, which is connected to consciousness of the soul, sees everything the physical mind cannot.

The signals the higher mind sends to the lower mind have different shapes and volumes. They can be sent in reality or through dreams. They can be weak and unclear feelings of foreboding, intuition; they can be sent to the physical mind as pictures and visions, seen in imagination; messages can be forwarded through some mediator, or via actions of another person (who is often unaware of their mediating role - but when mediators are animals, they are perfectly aware of their role); they can come through written or spoken words which we hear or read at the right moment, on a billboard or in the Bible; we experience a miraculous synchronicity of events. Actually, synchronicity is very often a method for sending messages from the higher mind and soul to our limited physical mind. In any case, if the higher consciousness estimates that the physical mind is capable of noticing and recognizing synchronicity without interpreting it as coincidence, everything can be finalized. At long last, consciousness of the soul can, in the rare instances when life of the physical body is in danger, or if the predicted path of development of life is at risk, implement tougher measures; it can clearly and loudly appear and if required express in words what the mind should know. This can be heard as a clear voice, sometimes in the head, or occasionally near the ear, or away from oneself, as if coming from a distance.

If necessary, the higher consciousness will push the body with physical force; if a man with a limited physical mind starts going the wrong way, leading to jeopardy, and if the soul estimates that neither intuition nor inspiration will help, and that voices will be misinterpreted, and if there is no mediator close at hand to help, the soul can cause a physical effect to stop the body going in the wrong direction. Maybe it will cause the man to trip while walking, at the perfect moment, or cause a minor injury; or it will simply push him back like some invisible force - this happened to one of my friends, a person with a good soul. Scared, she went back, and managed to avoid gruesome consequences. Such interventions can go all the way to teleportation. This happened to Helena Blavatsky (Helena Petrovna Blavatsky), a great soul who conveyed important information from the higher spheres to this world, and is the founder of the Theosophical Society. On one occasion, she found herself in a life-threatening situation during violent street demonstrations, and she was suddenly teleported to a quiet back street.

Consciousness of the soul can act as an unexpected force that suddenly arises and makes matters better.

The closer we are to consciousness of the soul, the clearer it is that we do not live in a material world where events happen mechanically or accidentally. A good percentage of events may be so, because it is necessary for the diversity of nature, but it becomes clearer that the divine consciousness of the soul can always act and handle any situation, including people, animals and events, to synchronize them when needed and to direct the unique drama of life, in which the divine consciousness is the director, the scriptwriter, the stuntman, and the theatre, all in one.

The more we become alienated from our own soul and identify with the mind, the more the world seems alienated; events appear mechanical and random, contradicting our being and life, and we are in conflict with nature and other people, with ourselves even. Materialists are people who are not sufficiently in possession of consciousness of their soul.

When we turn to ourselves, to consciousness of our soul, to the divine consciousness, then it also turns to us. **This happens automatically, in parallel, like a mirror reflection.** Existence reveals itself to us more and more as a living and omnipresent force, like unconditional love. When in meditation we begin to feel a clear consciousness of ourselves for the first time, consciousness of our soul, then the divine whole responds to our consciousness with many challenges, which have one goal only: to strengthen our consciousness, to clear it from illusions. The clearer our self-consciousness is in meditation, the easier it is to see that all of the difficulties and challenges that come our way are the elixir which purifies our self-consciousness, the elixir which changes all events, the states of diseases, confrontation and slavery, and transforms them into health, understanding and freedom. But elixirs often work through nasty side effects such as diarrhea and other forms of uncomfortable cleansing of the organism. When we turn to ourselves, to our soul, when we correctly practise meditation, all ostensible conflicts and challenges turn into the dialectics of our awareness of ourselves. The more meditation seems impure and far from us, the more challenges of life and the adversity we experience act as an impediment to our practice of meditation. Only in the purest meditative awareness of ourselves can we see that the divine whole, like a mother, always welcomes us joyfully, when we remember to turn to it, towards ourselves and our soul. It communicates with us through all events, in order to recognize and realize itself using our consciousness. It is happy for us, and keeps smiling while we go through life, in the same way a mother does to a child who is waking.

When man's reasoning is based on the lower mind and ego only, he makes judgments based on power and self-interest, because at the base of his deduction is a tendency towards preservation of the ego, an attempt to defend himself from the unknown, and also to a large degree ignorance and distrust toward higher forces and consciousness of the soul. He lives in fear of his survival, which he sees only in the physical reality around himself; all his actions are based on this fear for his existence. These are the people who have no belief in the soul, in the afterlife and in God. They are unscrupulous fighters for their own interests and do not know forgiveness and mercy. They trade with everything they have and do, even with their own feelings, because they always take everything they can get from other people. Such people are capable of committing physical violence.

All mercy and kindness come to this world from consciousness of the soul; every act of peace and tranquility brings awareness to the fact that the body is not all that exists, that life itself and existence surpass the body and the current contents of the mind, that everything is interconnected by a higher, common factor. The presence of love and serenity of forgiveness is a sure compass that unmistakably points to the presence of consciousness of the soul, or to the absence of the former, when the physical mind and ego are in charge and using crudeness and violence and calculated dealership.

The spirituality that enables the consciousness of the soul to overcome the mind is also a source of great wit and humour. A sense of humour which prevails in all circumstances, even those that prove to be the hardest for man, is a reflection of consciousness of the soul, which is always above events and conditioning of the mind and the body. Wit is the ability to connect two seemingly incompatible notions (which is generally inconceivable for the conditioned mind); the ability to see things and events from a higher perspective and dimension than the standard one, independently of space and time. Wit is an act of fooling around with the illusions that limit the mind. This is why truly spiritual people can always be recognized as being funny and witty most of the time. Spirituality without a sense of humour is only numbness of the mind. Soulless people do not possess any sense of humour.

Due to the illusion of separation from the divine source, all people feel loneliness and alienation in this world. But it is only a state of ostensible separateness of the physical mind from the higher mind and consciousness of the soul. That ostensible separateness is the cause of all negativity in the world, in individuals and between people. This ostensible separateness from the divine source also generates a true urge to reach unity with it; it further establishes the creative potential of consciousness in man, to inspire him to return to his original state of the divine soul and which naturally understands reality. Because of the illusion of separation from the soul, people seek sanctuary in a variety of ways and in diverse forms, from creating better living conditions, to developing creativity to improve and upgrade things - which all results in superior civilizations and cultures; we also seek perfection in relationships with other people - conflicts and misunderstandings are only part of this complex process; until finally we begin to seek sanctuary in the meaning of existence. The tendency towards unity with the divine source is the real base of love and creativity. It is the driving force of all civilizations and cultures. It is the essential aspiration of all our incarnations. The essence of this tendency is in connecting the mind in the physical body to the higher mind and consciousness of the soul, and consequently, by means of it, with the divine source of everything. This is the only act people actually perform during their lifetime, through all their incarnations. Only in the connection with consciousness of the soul do people experience real freedom, understanding and true sanctuary.

* * *

Such connectedness between the mind and consciousness of the soul is directly accomplished through meditation. Meditation has always existed so that people are able to realize a direct connectedness with the soul. All our lives are dedicated to this, however without meditation that connectedness takes far longer to realize, and the path is undoubtedly steeper.

Man's growth in consciousness and awareness is the growth of the presence of consciousness of the soul in the body. Although it cannot embody it in its entirety, it can increase its presence in the physical body to the point where the body transforms into light. Even so, the presence of consciousness of the soul in man is clearly visible in the form of kindness, love, wisdom and enlightenment.

It should come across here that the relationship between the mind in the body and consciousness of the soul operates in parallel realities which are simultaneous. This means that we can transform from a state of being closed off into the body, mind and ego, to transcendental consciousness of the soul, but only if the appropriate incentives are provided. There are no external limitations that prevent this from happening, merely subjective limitations of the mind itself, for it is only the mind that slams the door shut to freedom on the inside. However, the relationship of the mind in the body and the soul represents the full spectrum of all potentials of human experiences, all human dramas and everything that constitutes this world that man has constructed in his inert physical reality. Several lives are needed for people to be able to cross over, away from the spectrum. More often than not, one human life may represent being stuck in one type of experience, and activate only a very small percentage of the range of experiences from the spectrum. Every man lives on a certain frequency of consciousness between the mind in the body and consciousness of the soul, keeping his distance from one or other reality. He can spend his entire life in only one frequency of that spectrum, experiencing all of its possibilities, but he can also progress towards higher frequencies during the course of his life, making an upward or a downward turn. This depends on his karmic maturity, or the level of maturity of the incarnation cycle he finds himself in. There are people who spend one entire life static on one level of consciousness, distant from consciousness of the soul, and there are people who leap forward-backward in one life, experiencing different states of consciousness and by doing so, they make headway towards greater consciousness of the soul. In reality, there are as many ways of freeing ourselves from the illusions of the mind and the limitations of the body, and opening ourselves to consciousness of the soul, as there are people in this world. The process is purely individual.

However, all people can only access one direct path, and that path is meditation.

Consciousness of the soul and the higher mind become stronger through discipline, the discipline of meditation, and also through an overall positive attitude toward life, which creates the conditions for establishing a closer contact with the consciousness that's the essence of life, and that is the consciousness of our soul. ***There is no other consciousness in existence. It is everywhere, one and the same, however it is used and expressed individually.*** If we accept it with a positive attitude in ourselves, and express it through ourselves, then we will come closer to that same consciousness that enables everything. In the same way, we will reach understanding of everything, both ourselves and the world.

The most convincing way of expressing the connection between the mind and consciousness of the soul, which a person does not realize in meditation or via unconditional love, though both serve as the correct paths to God, is through conscientiousness and righteousness. ***The ability to act in accordance with our conscience and with a sense of justice is the ability to rely on consciousness of the higher mind, and consciousness of the soul.*** This is why conscientiousness is always a reflection of proper action; the power of consciousness of the soul that expresses itself in such a manner may occasionally call for some sacrifice, sometimes even self-sacrifice. All those people who chose to sacrifice their own life rather than compromise their conscience have firmly established a bond with consciousness of their soul. Languages use assorted terms to convey this, such as 'they have not sinned' or 'they have saved their soul'.

Those who have made a mistake and come into conflict with their own conscientiousness, with the consciousness of their soul, can use that mistake to further strengthen consciousness of the soul and realize the importance of its preservation. They are eager to redeem themselves for the mistake they've made, in order to 'ease their conscience', so that their 'conscience is clear'.

A person with strong consciousness of the soul, that is with a strong conscience, always acts righteously and honestly; for him this is the only way to be and act, the only way to live. Improper things he views as abnormal and unbearable, counteracting life. He does not require the morals or ethics that popular religions preach to know what to do, or what is right. He is self-reliant and self-sufficient, because he acts from the consciousness of his soul. He is the role model for morality and ethics, regardless of the religion he was born into or his level of education.

Morals, ethics and culture actually exist only as a weak external replacement for consciousness of the soul, which is the only route in this world that yields what is good and right; these external replacements exist to young and immature people, until they reach consciousness of the soul to a sufficient degree that they can act of their own accord. Without consciousness of the soul, morals, ethics and culture can be, and often are, misused.

Every single man, as well as all of mankind, mature in such a way that they enable consciousness of the soul to implement itself, unhindered by outside factors.

When the soul is given permission to do as it sees fit, without distraction, a phenomenon happens within the body of this karmically mature and enlightened individual, and this person radiates about himself bliss and benevolence which can be felt in his presence quite clearly.

Conscience is connected with memory, and the nature of memory can be clear to us only in the context of understanding the quantum field (*akasha*), consciousness and the mind. We have said that in the universal field, *akasha*, or the quantum field, everything is already present in its potential or unmanifested state. This is the universal divine consciousness before its manifestation into existence, into the cosmos as we know it. All of the consciousness which exists in nature is the same consciousness that has its origin in *akasha*, the quantum field. All of our memories come from there. Memory is not located somewhere in the brain; the brain only serves the purpose of oblivion of the quantum consciousness, for the seeming separation from the current timeless connectedness of everything into one whole. **All of memory is actually only a partial connectedness of the mind with the universal quantum field in which everything already exists, with akasha, where everything is already stored.** Ancient knowledge tells us this; it teaches us of the 'chronicles of *akasha*' in which everything timeless is 'written', everything that was, is and will be. This is why after the death of the body, when we approach consciousness of the soul which is one with the universal field, *akasha*, we are faced with that consciousness, and we go through every detail of our life in one timeless moment. That has further introduced the idea of 'judgment day'; something the controllers of our mind scare us with. Telepathy and supernatural perception are based on this. It is nothing but the connectedness of our mind to the quantum field in which everything already exists, the connection of the mind with consciousness of the soul that resides in that field. The more our consciousness relies on this field, the more it is able to perceive than if it were restricted to the physical body alone.

The entire manifested cosmos is contained within the quantum field (*akasha*, ether), and the connection of our mind with this universal field is what we call 'memory'; nothing comes about as if new in existence, it only gets manifested from a concealed state into a revealed one. The nature of existence equals the complete absence of non-existence. The universe is a hologram of the quantum field into which nothing can disappear; everything exists in its timeless form in perpetual existence; **all the diversity of existence is based on the alternating phases in the manifestation between the concealed and the revealed state, and the perception of that difference.** In doing so, **observation has a reverse effect on manifestation**. In such a way, consciousness and existence come full circle. In human experience this law is evident in the law of karma, where everyone is faced with the consequences of their actions and misconduct. Nobody escapes the outcome of their actions, in the same way that nobody can escape themselves. A man is known for his actions. Such is the nature of this holographic universe: everything is contained within everything.

Probably the most convincing expression of consciousness of the soul is spontaneity. Spontaneity and honesty in our actions are the most obvious in children. With children, consciousness of the soul is most visible, simply because the body of a child is small and still untainted by karmic actions; consciousness of the soul does not grow at the same pace as the body, it always possesses one stable quality, and it is much bigger than the physical body. For this reason, children radiate spirituality, because it is much greater than them. They radiate bliss, laughter, spontaneity and playfulness, for no special reason. This is the characteristic of soulful people and soulful nations. Spontaneity is connected with the joy of life. Spontaneity can be appealing, because consciousness of the soul is extremely inviting, but it can be to the point of suppressing rationality. This is an occurrence that happens too often. With children, it is regulated by upbringing and learning, but with nations and societies which are prone to spontaneous living, a lack of rationality in the culture of living and working tends to prevail. On the other hand, there are societies such as Anglo-Saxon and Protestant ones, which greatly emphasize rationality in the culture of living, and therefore suppress spontaneity, and together with it the quality of soulfulness. It requires great wisdom to find the right balance between these opposites, spontaneous wholeheartedness and rationality in one's accomplishments in the world. This is the true goal of the birth of the soul. So it should be the final goal of every culture.

Meditation is nothing but the skill of achieving the ideal balance between consciousness of the soul and one's overall actions in this world, using body and mind.

All of the diversity in life experiences is a game of the lower mind, which in this world lives like in a dream. In reality, we can never lose consciousness of our soul, we do not have a hold over it; consciousness of our soul has a controlling influence over us, our entire being and our life, and stays very close. Nature is its imagination. Everything that happens is the divine consciousness of the soul trying out and experimenting with no limits; scenario one of this is the utter oblivion of itself. In order to realize oblivion of itself, it has constructed this type of physical body, a place in which to reside, but also in which it will forget itself. This is why the body has energy centres or chakras, which represent subordination of the state of consciousness, from the highest to the lowest.

Beneath the physical or empirical mind, consciousness is limited even further in the psycho-energetic centres or chakras. All of the chakras represent states of consciousness, as existential states. They are all the levels on which we can exist, starting from the rudimentary instinctive (first chakra), all the way up to the greatest openness toward consciousness of the soul and the divine consciousness (in the highest, seventh chakra).[2]

Consciousness of the soul slows as it descends to the lower mind and body, where it gradually gets rougher, down to the lower psycho-energetic centres or chakras. ***The body, brain and mind are nothing but mechanisms which enable the slowing of divine consciousness of the soul.*** It is current, much like the 'divine particle', which instantly keeps creating all of existence, all the cosmos and all of life. All current happenings and relations are, when objectively observed, current and timeless. ***The body slows down the speed to a level where that which is essentially timeless becomes in time, so we are able to observe it in our linear time;*** the vibrations of the 'divine particle' which exceed the speed of light are momentary and omnipresent, ***and we see them as an inert object in time and space, separate and distinct from other objects. This kind of slow perception creates our nervous system. The brain and nervous system, therefore, do not serve to produce consciousness, but on the contrary, to slow it and numb it to a sufficient degree that we do not perceive the***

---

[2] On chakras and states of consciousness, see my book 'Samadhi - Unity of Consciousness and Existence.'

timeless divine presence, which is always in the current moment, but instead the alienated world of objects set in space and time. **To perceive only existence and not consciousness**, and not the divine Absolute, so that consciousness seems separated from existence, conquered by the divine Absolute. This is because the nervous system and the brain only slow down and limit consciousness. Once we overcome the limiting conditioning of the body and brain, whether with transcendence in meditation or with death of the body, an out-of-body experience, a narcotic or similar, we automatically experience an expanded consciousness and we are faced with the timeless presence of the divine consciousness of the Absolute. All of this contradicts the concepts of mainstream science which state that consciousness arises from dead matter. This is very important to remember, because it will be the basis for understanding the practice of meditation.

Such is the structure of our being.

This is why the highest divine inspiration resides in it, as well as the lowest instincts and the struggle for survival. Hence, all the conflicts and discrepancies within human beings.

The reason for everything being the way it is in the already stated tendency of the divine Absolute to experience all of its options, and in order to succeed in this it has to create its own opposition: an individual consciousness which will seemingly be separate from itself, from the divine whole. This is man's physical mind in the body, or what we know as ego. Only when consciousness of the soul reaches it, will all the possibilities of the divine presence become truly known, since the divine consciousness is omnipresent, always and everywhere, even in the most unlikely phenomenon, completely alienated from existence. An example of this would be one materialistic scientist who believes in neither God nor the soul.

Understanding the structure of human beings is necessary in order to understand the structure of the practice of meditation. Indeed, the structure and mechanism of the practice of meditation cannot differ from the structure and functioning of our being. They have to be in unison and well-harmonized, because otherwise meditation would not serve the purpose of our being. Meditation which is different from the structure of our being would actually be a method of alienation from ourselves and the divine essence; sadly such meditative techniques are in operation. The temptations of contrary things exist in everything, even in the techniques of meditation.

The structure of our being, which we have described as separated into the lower and higher mind, can be correctly understood through the nature of different frequencies. Everything exists in vibrations, starting with the primary vibration of the Absolute into its opposite point or 'divine particle', which in turn creates all other vibrations, all the way down to the roughest or slowest, which we perceive as the physical world. Every phenomenon originates as a vibration. All phenomena are just vibrations, nothing else; nothing is substantial.

When we meditate, we change vibrations; we calm our being, making its vibrations finer or more subtle. In this way, through meditation we move from the rough towards the fine and the subtle, from a lower state of consciousness to a higher; practically this means that we cross over from consciousness of the rough mind in the body to consciousness of the higher mind and consciousness of the soul (from Hertzian to non-Hertzian frequencies).

The way we vibrate is the way we get around in the world. When we vibrate roughly (in Hertzian frequencies) then we are in a rough body and are experiencing rough experiences, full of contradictions and challenges. When we vibrate in a finer way (via non-Hertzian frequencies) then we are in higher vibrations which exchange information in a more rapid manner; the vibrations of the higher mind experience better quality events by compressing them in time and space, and exchanging them immediately, while also inspecting them from all sides to discover their meaning. When vibrations of our being (body-mind) become the finest, equating to the maximum level of comprehension possible while we are in a physical body, then we are in meditation, and we become open to a higher consciousness of our soul. The higher consciousness of our soul cannot enter our mind when it is occupied with rough vibrations it takes from the even rougher body. The body and mind must be made still and distance from rough vibrations, in order for the finest vibrations of our soul to reach our body and penetrate the mind.

This is why meditation is, in effect, the stillness of one's entire being, body and mind. When the stillness our being becomes subtle and fine to a sufficient degree for consciousness of a transcendental soul to reach it and to permeate it enough to gain control, it is a way in which the structure of our being coincides with the functioning of meditative practice.

Stillness in meditation gradually gets easier to achieve as consciousness of the soul penetrates ever more through the finer layers, into the body and mind. Namely, man grows in the awareness that any movement, from the primary transformation of the Absolute into one particle (the circle into the point), to every single movement of our mind, means eventually arriving at the same destination in the divine consciousness, in its absolute essence. Everything moves in this direction, all of the cosmos, all of life, all beings, all human destinies, all efforts and all dreams. All is one joint movement travelling toward its outcome. The movements of our mind and body are no different from the movements of the universe, the Absolute itself, because the universe is a hologram, so absolutely nothing in it is separated, everything is actually one and the same movement which is divided and multiplied fractally in accordance with the golden cross-section.

When we transform our consciousness into a thought, and keep on doing so every moment we are not completely aware of ourselves, we have mimicked the Absolute when it projected itself into a point, the 'divine particle' and into the entire manifested world. This is why the origin of thought is identical to the origin of the manifested world. With the disappearance of thoughts, the manifested world also disappears.

Only once we are able to catch a glimpse of this - even if only for a second - can we truly be calm and relaxed in meditation. Meditation is nothing but a type of insight, the expansion and a way of determining such insight.

But, surely, the purpose of everything is not for everything to stop, to return to its absolute outcome in order to cease. Only the relative mind could come up with such a false notion. In accordance with everything we have said on the nature of the Absolute and its manifested existence, the purpose of everything is that in each manifested moment and shape of existence, the divine Absolute is recognized as such. For the difference between the unmanifested and manifested Absolute and movement and calmness to disappear, a clear conscience is needed, one that has been purified of all discrepancies of manifested existence; the type of consciousness that exceeds any differentiation. In reality, there never was any difference between the unmanifested and manifested, the Absolute and the relative aspect of the divine. Nor can there be. The difference exists only in the mind that is unaware of its own true nature, the source of its consciousness, and that is the mind that has never experienced meditation. All the perceived differences are only projections of the mind.

Only when we truly experience the divine consciousness as our essence will we cease to see a difference between meditation and each movement of being, both our own and the cosmos. Our meditation will be the union of our consciousness with the common movement of existence, unmistakably centred in its own divine outcome. Such transcendental consciousness brings forth an overcoming of time. In it, movement and the resting are absolutely one and the same. Overcoming time provides the insight that each moment is eternal, that every shape is the void of the divine Absolute, that every movement is actually the happening of the divine within itself; each movement of the cosmos, from atoms to galaxies, is nothing but the manner in which the consciousness of the divine Absolute actualizes and establishes itself within itself; that its reality was not, nor will it ever be in the future; it is always here and now, there is only the present moment which is taking place within itself, in all possible ways.

Having in mind the structure of our being and meditation, as well as the relationship between the mind and consciousness of the soul, a careful reader will notice that something is amiss; something does not add up to the traditional teaching of meditation. We aim to present Buddhist meditation in a detailed manner here, from early Buddhist teachings, whilst, at the same time, talking about consciousness of the soul and the divine Absolute; man makes this connection in meditation. The interpretation of Buddhism which has reached us and which is now taught in the world states that Buddha did not teach about the soul and the divine, about the Absolute. True enough, Buddha did not use these terms, but in many of his speeches he described out-of-body states and after-death experiences, all of which implies that consciousness is exalted and more permanent than the body. In Buddha's time, there was chaos in religious and metaphysical teachings, ranging from the darkest materialism and demonism to the highest idealism and blind faith, which brought about worship of various deities, and even the belief in nothingness. Buddha renounced all the teachings of his age and addressed them with due criticism. One example is enough; Buddha argued with a man who believed that he would achieve immortality of his soul if he started mimicking a dog (*Kukkuravatika Sutta, Majjhima Nikaya* 57). Just this one example makes it clear the level of understanding of the soul he encountered in his day, and what he had to renounce.

    Buddha was a hygienist of suffering; his teaching is the discipline of awakening man from all the limitations of body and mind, rather than metaphysical teaching which would deceive man and waste his time. This is why he did not speak openly about the soul, divine consciousness and the Absolute, since the non-awakened man would find it too easy to hold on to these concepts and turn them into a religion to worship, instead of acquiring the proper understanding of them as guidelines for practice on the path to his own self-realization. Buddha knew better than to talk of the goal to the one who had not reached the goal, because it would be counterproductive; the mind always presents it as though it were already in possession of it.[3] How a mind deceives us will be covered in the next chapter. To convince someone who is totally identified with the mind that he has an immortal soul is counterproductive, because he then stops the effort of making his soul conscious, because consciousness is essentially a property of the soul, consciousness originates from the soul. The soul came to the body to achieve its full potential of awareness of itself. It is much better to say to such a man that he needs to become aware, and to show him how to do that. For this reason, Buddha always spoke of the method and discipline that helped others reach the goal, and he discouraged dealing with metaphysical issues which drive people to confusion, or to think they have already reached their intended goal. People are inclined to project the questions of their essence and consciousness into metaphysics, and turn them into an object of worship. The same is true today with all people; everybody is aware of the words 'God' and 'soul' and everybody thinks that they know what these mean, in the same way they know the shoes they wear every day. But how do they go about in real life, in existence and toward other people? In a way quite contrary to the conduct of a man aware of God and souls. Actually, those who call out God the loudest, kill in his name the most. Buddha foresaw religious fundamentalism. Being awakened, he knew too well to what degree people were unconscious. That is why he did not speak openly about the soul and the divine reality, but only about the path to the awareness.

---

[3] On all the pitfalls of these mental projections see the book by Jiddu Krishnamurti: "The First and Last Freedom".

Early Buddhism, in the first centuries AD, was just this: a path of purifying (*Visuddhimaggo*). It was not an organized religion, but a well-harmonized community where everyone worked on themselves, on purifying their being from everything that conditions the consciousness and wakefulness. What is an impurity that's purified through that purification? We have seen that it is the body with the mind. What should be cleansed in that purification? We have seen that it is consciousness of the soul. This is the only thing that enables everything. There is no other consciousness. Buddhism got its name from the term 'awaken'. What would the term 'awakening' refer to, if not the consciousness that enables existence? The awakening is the consciousness. The soul is the source, which acts as the carrier of the divine consciousness in an individual being. Buddhists are non-violent in their relationships with all living beings not out of goodness, but because they see one and the same consciousness of the divine soul in all beings. Only those who are not aware of their soul can kill.

Everything that Buddha negates in his speeches, that relate to something permanent in man, are the factors that compose a being in this world; or, to be more precise, the five *skandhas*: the material shape of the body (*rŭpa-skandhâ*), sensory abilities (*vedana skandhâ*), observations (*samđna*), expressing stimuli or will for a reactive action (*karmendriye*), and the mind (*manas*) - actually, the identification with the mind. Nothing else. He clearly reveals their conditionality, inconstancy and transience. For all these factors of existence, he advises that one rise in awareness, with full alertness, and perceive all five as different from ourselves; he teaches how to distinguish between all the factors of our being and our consciousness, which he put concisely as: 'This is not me, this is not mine, this I am not'. Buddha repeated this formulation in his speeches on meditation. It is exactly what is seen by knowing that consciousness of the soul overcomes all and transcends all. *Were it not for consciousness that overcomes and transcends all, not even Buddha could become aware of the true nature of the composing factors of a being.* The consciousness which overcomes everything transient, and owing to which we can become aware of the transience, together with every object of perception, is the only correct representation of the soul. However, those five *skandhas* were considered to be (in Buddha's day) the true characteristic of human essence, *atta* or *atma*, which in metaphysical speculations is identified with the soul. Even today, psychologists do the same when they identify the soul with psychophysical functions of the body and mind. Buddha criticized and renounced such speculations.

In *Sutta-nipato*, 1076, Buddha states positively that for one who has attained the ultimate purpose, *nirvana*, it cannot be said that he does not exist, but that no criteria of this world applies to him any longer. He emphasizes that death is neither a solution nor a *nirvana*, and therefore it is clear that there is something which goes from life to life, and which has to be purified in order to reach *nirvana*.

Buddha stated many times that his path leads from the centre, placed in between all the opposing sides, between the extremes of nihilism, which he condemned, and eternalism, the mental conviction in the eternity of anything. His path is the path of rationality, of perceiving reality here and now, as it is in itself, and not what we imagine it to be.

Finally, the outline of Buddha's teaching on the essence of existence of human beings is the concept of void

(Pali: *sunnam*, Sanskrit: *sunyam*). That is, however, the same term which was used for the mathematical mark zero in his time. Buddha, therefore, spoke of 'nullity' and not about negation or nothingness; he spoke of the zero state in the same way in which we described the non-Hertzian properties of the unmanifested (quantum) aspect of existence and consciousness. We described the concept of zero at the beginning of this book as the essential characteristic of the divine Absolute. The zero contains no negation of anything; it rather represents the basis for all other numbers, or sizes. This is the only correct way in which the Absolute can be understood. Everything else is the metaphysics of an unenlightened mind.

All the consequences of an awakening following the practice of Buddhist meditation clearly show that the game is only about consciousness of the soul wishing to express itself completely, in this world and in the body. A Buddhist who is awakened treats his body, mind and the world in an identical manner to the consciousness of the soul. If you want to see what completely purified consciousness of the soul, fully realized itself in this world looks like in the body, look closely at Buddha and Buddhist saints, their behavior and conduct.

However, there are forces in this world that deal with concealing consciousness of the soul and consciousness of the divine reality. These forces falsely represent Buddha's teaching as religion without a soul' and 'teaching about nothingness'.

WHY DOES THE MIND KEEP DECEIVING US EVEN AS IT AWAKENS US

We are all too familiar with stories that the illusion of the world is in the mind; this is called maya. The fact remains that the mind, with all its lucidity and intelligence, can participate in the most atrocious evil, but also the greatest good, that it may equal creation and destruction, depending on the mood. In fact, all of meditation consists of overcoming and transcending the mind, for one simple reason: it is the primary condition for self-awareness; and yet, without the mind, we are lost in the world and are unable to reach meditation.

Why is this so?

Because the mind is perfect in its performance.

It is the most perfect part of the human being, a tiny reflection of the perfection of the divine consciousness. Consciousness is one and the same in everything, and we, both in the body and mind, use only a fraction of it. Consciousness acts like a mirror, it enables the perception of all happenings and all potential happenings. ***And the mind acts like a mirror.*** That is why it is so clear and so neutral in its performance.

In accordance with the dimensions of existence, the mind belongs to the element of air, which is at the top of the pyramidal structure of existence; time and space overlap there. All of the lower dimensions represent the progressive increase of manifestation of time and space. In the element of air (or the mind), time and space of all events are joined in the here and now. That is why in the mind we can imagine any event virtually, here and now, independently of time and space, and we can design and understand the past and the future, the distant and the close. ***The mind is virtual reality.*** As such, it is an extremely useful tool - the most useful in existence. The mind is possible because the universe is a hologram; in each, even in the smallest part, everything is reflected, the whole. In this way, we can see the wholeness of the universe and get to know all its laws in our mind.

If general manifested existence is the mirror for consciousness of the Absolute of itself, then our minds are a small part of that mirror. The problem lies in the fact that a mind does its job impeccably, it perfectly reflects reality in its virtual way. Then we come to a paradox: with the help of the mind we get closer to perception of reality, and the clearer we see it in our virtual manner, the more real it looks; that is, the virtual reality of our mind looks like reality; the closer we are to that mirror, the clearer we see manifested reality.

This is where the paradox happens: the clearer the mind virtually perceives reality, the less different reality is from its virtual reflection in the mind. A subtle replacement of the virtual reality with true objective reality takes place, due to the proximity and clarity of the reflection of reality within the mind. The closer we are to insight into reality, the more we are convinced that we have already achieved it. However, it never comes to the connection of mind with reality. The mind can approach reality up to 99%, but the interval of 1% always stays, as long as the mind persists. This is because the very proximity and clarity of reality in the mind provides the illusion that it all adds up to 100% of reality, that reality itself has already been achieved in the mind. Therefore, it is possible that an individual is mentally convinced of something, despite having no personal experience of it consequently, the more he knows something, the firmer the illusion holds. That is why there is a difference between objective and subjective reality. That is why the man in question never becomes reality itself, but rather stays in the virtual reality of his mind, which, due to the perfect performance of the mind in its capacity to mirror reality, looks the same - looks like reality itself.

This paradox is inevitable because of the nature of the mind and the nature of reality.

Substituting the true reality with virtual reality is the foundation for all the illusions people live in.

The mind is a virtual reality that can do everything, mimic a dreamlike state while at the same time actively experiencing reality in the physical world, appear completely rational, or end up under a complete misapprehension. People with such minds live their entire life like in a dream. In that dream they are able to learn and work, explore the world of politics and science, they can even construct a religion from their own vision of reality (all religions are visions which substitute reality). The mind will do everything to justify itself and its virtual reality. Virtual reality of the mind is capable of doing everything, of reflecting the most supreme divine reality whilst simultaneously remaining under the illusion that it is separate from the divine consciousness which is everything, failing to see or experience it. The paradoxical state of mind makes the paradox look normal. The mind will elegantly, with all scientific, religious and philosophical arguments, discard all the evidence of its paradoxical state. The mind sees the paradox only when it suits it.

This is the exact definition of illusion and life asleep: not being aware that the only reality is the divine consciousness which is the true nature of existence, far greater than mere sensory observation.

For man to overcome this paradox of the mind, to transfer from his virtual mental reality to actual reality, a leap is needed which, for the mind, looks like a jump over an abyss, like a little death. All initiations which contain the experience of death and rebirth are related to the overcoming of the paradox of the mind. This leap is the transcendence of the whole mind, which is possible only with perfect understanding of the operation of the whole mind, with the understanding which leads to transcendence; and that is not the analysis in which the mind keeps spinning round and playing with itself, but the testimony, the objective awakening by way of establishing every movement of the mind, every thought and the entire being. Likewise, this paradox of the mind can be overcome with complete surrender, giving up the mind and surrendering to the whole. Even though they look opposite, these two methods are essentially the same. Self-awareness of the mind corresponds to introverted people, who are karmically mature enough to be detached from the world, and surrendering belongs more to extroverts who still have karmic ties to the manifested world.

Every movement of the mind is the creation of virtual existence in time. That is what the mind does: it reflects existence in virtual time. It always pertains to the past and acquired experience. The mind is not created to see the future, to see the whole, it just keeps gathering impressions and reacting to them. Consciousness of the mind is different from consciousness of the soul in the respect that the mind is always a reaction and attached to the past, to already acquired impressions and habits. Consciousness of the soul is the exact opposite, it is independent of all impressions and it always gives insight into the whole, it is always positive in the same way that existence itself is fundamentally a positive phenomenon. The mind is always negative, but it can appear positive in those brief moments when it connects with consciousness of the soul. Consciousness of the soul opens us toward the eternal, i.e. the timeless reality which is here and now in everything; the mind torments us with its constant attachment to time, either with something bygone or yet-to-be. This is what distinguishes the mind action from the soul action. Since the mind is essentially negative and restricted, even though it is necessary for the understanding of the physical world, the arduous task of consciousness of the soul attempting to sprout in the body and in physical reality is possible only when the mind is suppressed and calmed, using feelings, rather than common sense. Feelings are what connects us with consciousness of the soul; the mind deals with impressions and reassessing, with doubts. The feeling of connectedness with consciousness of the soul is the feeling when we absolutely know that we are right, and engrosses our entire being with bliss for having found ourselves, our true sanctuary and meaning.

Meditation is the method with which we purify and release our true feelings; we cleanse ourselves of the impact of the conditioned mind and thoughts, and switch over to feelings that connect us with consciousness of the soul. We come to those true feelings by setting the mind free from connectedness to objects and turning it toward its source, toward the consciousness which enables it, together with everything else. We aim it at consciousness of the soul. This is meditation.

It is easy to recognize those feelings the conditioned mind has influence over. These are all negative feelings, which split us from the whole, take us into conflict with other people and beings and with the whole itself, with existence. When we only feel what the mind and physical reality provide for us, then we endure a plight. This brings us in conflict with reality. When we are in conflict with reality, we want to abandon that state, but this wish occurs in our mind merely as a reaction to the negative state. In such a way, being in conflict with the present reality, we only multiply conflicts, we give off more energy so that the negative state prevails. Much like a tug of war, where we are opposed to the mind and negative feelings, therefore always in conflict with reality and suffering. The only way to get out of this negative state is not to resist it with sheer reaction only, striving to something better based on the rejection of the present, because then, as a consequence, we give off energy focusing on the things we do not want, which leaves us internally split and stuck in one place. We ought to grow in understanding that everything is a whole, which we are a part of, that it is us doing it to ourselves, to try to make a conscious effort to be positive unconditionally, because it is one and the same consciousness that constitutes all states, all of existence. If two men are in conflict, they use the same life energy and the same consciousness which enables everything. Reconciliation and overcoming all conflicts is only possible with the proper insight into that same common consciousness which begets them. We can reach this state only with meditation, which is the cessation of all conflicts and divisions within ourselves.

It is even easier to recognize those real feelings which connect us with consciousness of the soul, with the divine reality. They are much stronger in their intensity, they are perfectly positive, and always act toward connecting us with existence in various ways, through events, people and all beings. We always experience this as unconditional divine love. Our connection with the divine consciousness of the soul through feelings becomes complete when our actions start to be based on unconditional love only. When we do unto others what we want others to do unto us. This also happens when we conform our mind into harmonization with the feelings which fill us with bliss and purpose. Such harmonization of mind and correct feelings, which we have from consciousness of the soul, happens only with the discipline of meditation, with which we calm down the self-will of the mind, with the transcendence of the mind. In order to reach consciousness of the soul, it is not necessary to do anything with the mind, because it always does everything in its power to preserve itself; we only need to calm the mind. The mind is calmed with the insight that we are not the mind, and by becoming so calm during meditation throughout our entire being, to the point that we clearly see the mind active within us, like some foreign object previously installed in us. If we remain independent and sufficiently calm to attain our true state, the mind will calm by itself, because we will stop giving it energy to identify with the mind. Likewise, the mind works based on past experiences and its connection to the past, to time; in order to reach transcendence, it is necessary to acknowledge the experience of its limitation. Intelligence and karmic maturity serve this purpose, as well as the experience of suffering. When we acquire the knowledge of what we are not supposed to do, then we turn to things we need to do. Only when we experience all the opposites, can we then overcome them in transcendence, to have consciousness of the higher mind which is the witness of all possible states of the lower mind, in the body. Such testimony of transcendental consciousness is the essence of meditation.

The essence of meditation is in ceasing to distinguish between consciousness of one's soul, one's Self, and one Self. We project our consciousness and ourselves into some virtual reality. The Absolute does the same as it keeps projecting itself into one point or 'divine particle' in every single moment, into the manifested cosmos. This is the same event taking place in different proportions, in the macrocosm and microcosm.

We differentiate our essence from ourselves in every single moment, much in the same way the Absolute does when it projects itself into the cosmos. The dream or illusion in which man lives in this world is made up of the same projections. We are, therefore, alienated from ourselves. The essence of meditation and wakefulness lies in the recognition that we are that consciousness with which we are aware of everything, with which we exist at all; the essence is in merging into the union with ourselves, with the consciousness which enables everything, because there is not a multitude of consciousnesses. In the same way, the essence of existence is in the fact that despite the fact that the Absolute keeps projecting itself into a cosmos in the form of multiple phenomena, nothing can be different from the Absolute for a single moment. In this way, the knowing of 'I am That', that divine consciousness which is aware of itself, which enables everything, which is existence itself, the moment this stage is reached signifies the end of meditation. This is the true meaning of the statements 'be who you are' or 'be yourself', 'be your own', 'I am' or 'know thyself'; 'see oneself in everything and everything in oneself'.

The distinction between consciousness and the contents of consciousness is the beginning of meditation.

The cessation of every duality (advaita) between consciousness and the contents of consciousness is the end of meditation.

MEDITATION AND KARMIC MATURITY

The divine consciousness manifests itself into all the individual shapes that constitute all events. On the highest level, we have monads of divine consciousness that branch out, much like a tree. There is one beautiful parable in which the origin of the soul and consciousness is compared to a tree, placed upside down with its roots protruding to the sky and its branches and leaves lying on the ground. The common root of all of existence is in the sky, in the universal quantum field where everything emerges as individual phenomena in space and time. From that common divine root, individual monads of consciousness are developed in the form of the tree's branches, known as archangels and angels in esoteric knowledge; while here on earth, every conscious individual is a single leaf. These individual leaves are the individual souls, placed in each man. This is the structure of the existence of consciousness and of the human souls who are the conscious subjects perceiving existence; hence, everything exists because of these conscious subjects, to be experienced by them. Existence is the mirror in which the divine consciousness is reflected, the consciousness which is compressed and individualized in man.

In our highest form we, as souls, as monads of divine consciousness, have created this universe, and all the stars and galaxies. This is the roots and the tree trunk. With further individualization of consciousness, we created the planets and all organic life. These are the branches of the tree. In the end, we created everything so we can express our soul individually, in our individual being, the physical body. These are the leaves of our tree of life. An awakened man is the flower, and his consciousness is the fruit that contains and reflects the life of the entire tree.

This whole process takes place in order to implement the divine consciousness in all the possibilities of existence. Souls, as the principles of consciousness, raise the level of awareness of existence, of all its possibilities and options, and in this way they retrieve it to the divine as consciousness of oneself. Everything happens because of perception and self-awareness, in all proportions, from the most supreme divine to the lowest human; everything aspires to cognition and understanding of oneself and existence.

Human souls are the principles of the divine consciousness which engages in the ultimate contradiction with itself, with the chief goal of reaching oblivion of itself; it enters physical reality with the aim of realizing its fullest potential, to introduce divine consciousness to existence, and by doing so it connects existence with the divine. Souls are the bringers of light of consciousness, in all possible aspects of existence, in all potential phenomena, and they return the divine consciousness to itself; they help the divine consciousness express itself in all possible ways throughout existence. **The souls, on their own, do nothing but exist and witness phenomena. Everything happens so these souls can become witnesses, in their capacity as conscious subjects.** This is why everything that seems meaningless and evil is allowed to happen; the sole purpose is for an immortal soul to experience relative existence. The purpose is to establish, consciously, all the possibilities of existence, every event, every potential action. Perception is the purpose. It is the true meaning of all events. *Phenomena seem pointless or malevolent to us only if we look for meaning elsewhere, in some shape of existence, in an object, rather than in the conscious subject that everything exists for and that everything happens for.*

The meaning and problems of life cannot be understood on the level from which they are manifested (in the body and the physical world). They can be understood only from a higher perspective, from a wider context, from that which enables life and all its happenings, from consciousness of the soul that precedes physical birth and is completely independent of it. No shape of life can exist without purpose and meaning, and raising awareness of this meaning is impossible without a conscious subject who is independent of all shapes of life, without transcendental consciousness of the soul.

The soul is born into the body to experience something; not just one experience, but a series of meaningful experiences; each soul has one or more themes which it must experience in its physical life, never alone but in a synchronized manner, together with the other souls; this is not always a pre-planned experience, but instead allows for a great degree of chance and uncertainty. In the ongoing game between planned intention and coincidence and risk, consciousness of transcendental freedom and independence of the soul crystallizes - into consciousness which starts to make sense of it all.

The purpose of oblivion of consciousness of the soul while it resides in the body is to renew the divine consciousness, using man's level of awareness, and to introduce it to the world. Much like a biofeedback effect: the physical body and life on this planet affect the soul as DDFAO biofeedback does, to raise awareness of all its functions, for awareness of what the soul truly is before its birth into the body, and independently of it.

Likewise, oblivion of consciousness of the soul in the physical body adds further proof to the fact that birth in the body is not the beginning of life for man, but his decline into a lower state. Every human being is a 'fallen angel'. Some less so, and some more so. Remembering our divine origin and the state of our true nature, which man has always had in this world, and with his inner strength and creativity, he expresses himself through religions and creation. Man does not begin to exist with physical birth, but falls asleep and experiences the utter oblivion of himself. This is why every man's life can be reduced to a great awakening and revelation of himself. Testimony of man's soul in this world is carried out, authenticated and confirmed through work and creativity, through culture and civilization.

In this process there is progress so complex and extensive that a single witness is insufficient; rather, many are required simultaneously, which puts pressure on one soul to incarnate into physical reality multiple times. Each soul, therefore, has its own incarnation cycle.

At the beginning of such a cycle, throughout the first phase, a soul merely gathers experiences of existence through the course of its incarnations in the body. This gathering takes place by means of action and reaction, orchestrating some actions, then understanding the outcome of these actions, in every possible way. This is called karma. This initial phase of gathering experience is so strong and appealing that consciousness of the soul falls into oblivion of itself as soon as it finds itself incarnated in the body. The awareness of objects and experiences overpowers everything else. This oblivion is necessary for consciousness of the soul to take part in the game, as if it were real.

When it reaches a critical mass of experiences based on action and reaction, then it starts to connect existence with consciousness, with the conscious subject and its role in events, to further design existence and discover its purpose, to start to become aware that one and the same divine consciousness is at the base of all existence and all events.

When it has matured enough for this, it starts to overcome its identification with existence, while still residing in the body, and freeing itself from acquired impressions, so strengthening the presence of its independent consciousness, the consciousness of the soul in the body. **This is achieved through meditation.** With this it even overcomes karma, because it strengthens the consciousness which surpasses all opposites, the objective consciousness of the nature of reality. The more it overcomes attachment to impressions and its reaction to them, the more it solidifies the objective consciousness which it possessed prior to its incarnation in the body.

Once it manages to fully gain consciousness of its soul, which it has independently of the body, and all the limitations and temptations of the physical world, when it ceases to be born with oblivion of itself, then the cycle of incarnations is broken, and the soul goes back to its authentic, divine state.

Incarnations continue as long as there is the smallest possibility of forgetting the soul or awareness of oneself. Incarnations exist like tantric practices of experiencing consciousness of oneself in extreme situations. Life on planet earth is actually a training ground for souls to try to preserve and experience awareness of themselves, in all possible states and under all circumstances, even those that are most unnatural.[4] When consciousness of the soul cannot lose itself anymore, not even in the worst and most unbelievable experiences and states, then it has achieved permanent wakefulness or consciousness of itself - its transcendental divine essence - and then incarnations are no longer possible. The soul has learnt that nothing exists other than itself, nothing except the divine consciousness of itself, and that divine consciousness represents everything that can exist, within body or without, and in all dimensions.

Here are the three phases of the incarnation cycle of souls:

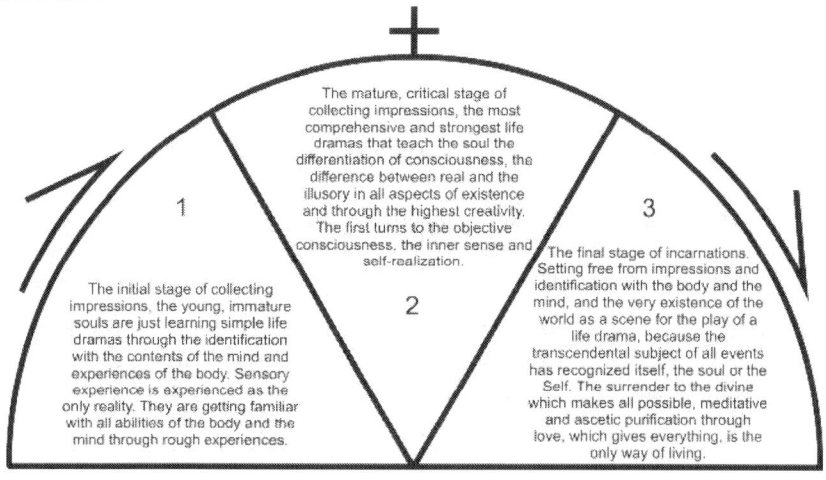

1 — The initial stage of collecting impressions, the young, immature souls are just learning simple life dramas through the identification with the contents of the mind and experiences of the body. Sensory experience is experienced as the only reality. They are getting familiar with all abilities of the body and the mind through rough experiences.

2 — The mature, critical stage of collecting impressions, the most comprehensive and strongest life dramas that teach the soul the differentiation of consciousness, the difference between real and the illusory in all aspects of existence and through the highest creativity. The first turns to the objective consciousness, the inner sense and self-realization.

3 — The final stage of incarnations. Setting free from impressions and identification with the body and the mind, and the very existence of the world as a scene for the play of a life drama, because the transcendental subject of all events has recognized itself, the soul or the Self. The surrender to the divine which makes all possible, meditative and ascetic purification through love, which gives everything, is the only way of living.

The horizon of karmic maturing through all incarnations of individual soul.

The second phase is critical: identification with the outer world of objects gradually ceases, thanks to consciousness of the soul reaching an acceptable level of maturity, resulting in inner maturity becoming more influential than the world of senses. Then, the first turning point from the outer to the inner takes place, at first only associatively and in the form of hints. These include all

---

[4] It can be said that for an individual soul, life in the body on earth bears a resemblance to the practice of *Aghori tantra*.

stories about the meaning of inner values, knowing ourselves, finding faith in ourselves and discovering our true worth, and finally about individuality and the process of individuality as a way to the Self. The critical element of this phase is characterized by an incompleteness in experience, in the partial abandonment of the world of illusions and insufficient knowledge of reality. One of the most difficult mistakes during this phase is the idealization of everything that the consciousness of the soul and the divine represent, and completely misunderstanding everything the physical world represents. Namely, the physical world is experienced as contrary to divine reality and the human soul, as something which is hostile to man, which enslaves man. The world is experienced as a very dark place which needs to be overcome. This is the tendency of some religions (Orthodox, Islam, Buddhism, Hinduism, Judaism). Even though insight into the world of illusions and nature which conditions man starts in this phase, there is not enough insight into reality, so you cannot perceive that the world is the true divine presence and its 'materialization'.

Gradually, over time, these hints ripen into a real soulfulness and wakefulness, a true turn to consciousness of oneself; that is, to one's soul. This change from the outer toward the inner, in the cycle of incarnation, can take place over the course of many lifetimes; nonetheless, it finally leads to the meditative discipline where it can realize itself. In meditation, identification with the external world is completely interrupted. Meditation represents the most concrete and final turning towards consciousness of our soul; in meditation the same turning which we experienced during many lives repeats itself, but without innuendoes and metaphors, without philosophy and religious distortions; in meditation we face the consciousness of our soul in a direct manner. This is why the cycle of incarnations is finalized with meditation. This is why only one who is mature enough for meditation can bring the cycle of his incarnation to the mature phase.

However, because the nature of existence is made up of all possible parallel realities, and has the property of timelessness, the time when we become mature enough for the final turning toward ourselves, toward consciousness of the soul, when we are mature enough for meditation, is in fact relative. There are no objective obstacles toward realizing all of that in the here and now, that works for each and every one of us, except the mental blocks which we maintain within ourselves. These obstacles are so strong that people spend multiple lives making an effort to turn towards their inner self, while at the same time reassuring themselves of the illusion of external objects.

The final purpose of turning to oneself and ending the cycle of incarnations is achieved after accomplishments in meditation, which means mastering and overcoming any connectedness to the world of objects - we know from the consciousness of our soul that there never existed a world of objects that we were supposed to respectively experience and renounce, that there is no difference between the outer world and inner consciousness of oneself, that the entire outer world is actually consciousness of the divine soul of itself, its actualization. We can no longer be born when we perceive that everything is the divine consciousness, even the roughest matter and the worst experiences in life. When we realize that everything is consciousness, we can no longer be unconscious. This is why we cease to be born into a body, because physical birth is nothing but a decline into a state of unconsciousness of consciousness of the soul, the divine consciousness that is all; a fall into the illusion that the world exists as some other quality.

All of the alertness and consciousness which man has in this world, all the happiness, bliss, and all the love, he gets from consciousness of his soul. All the suffering which man experiences in this world he gets from the loss of consciousness of his soul, of its eclipse.

Still, the greatest happiness and bliss can be experienced, while the soul still resides in physical reality, while at the same time being fully aware of itself, independent from the body and its current incarnation. This may only happen once it experiences all the aspects of existence, and learns how to set itself free from them. It liberates itself with the perfect understanding of their true nature, of the consciousness which is at the base of everything and which overcomes everything. At that breaking point, it receives the most wonderful blessing, because then, when it has completely regained consciousness of itself, even in the darkest areas of physical existence, the soul connects to its source, the divine consciousness of the Absolute, with all the possibilities of existence - even those options that seem the farthest from itself, with the physical reality as we know it.

When the soul experiences and connects with full awareness and understanding of the entire process; that is, when it removes all ostensible discrepancies of existence, then the divine consciousness reveals itself in existence as existence itself.

Then existence reveals itself as perfection, divine, here and now; the illusions of time and space disappear, and never again do they share our experience with the here and now. The present time of the perfect divine presence becomes the only possible reality for each and every moment for that soul, together with all the shapes of existence, always here and now.

With the practice of meditation, man through himself starts grounding the divine consciousness into existence, and through his experience and actions he achieves a primordial unity of divine consciousness and existence. The circle and the dot join in him, the Absolute together with all the manifested world. He starts acting using the divine consciousness. The divine consciousness acts through him. There is no difference or duality.

In the course of all its incarnations, the soul was preparing for such ability and such perfection - to be able to express through itself and its actions that unity of divine consciousness and existence. People are born and souls are incarnated for this very reason.

__Only those people whose souls have entered the final phase of incarnation, who are setting themselves free from impressions and previously conditioned reactions to events of the outside world, are actually mature enough for meditation, mature enough to stop looking at the outside world and to leave behind all the illusions of life, and allow the divine consciousness to start expressing through them.__

Only such people are able to perceive during meditation that the divine consciousness has always been happening, and that nothing else actually happens each moment. For them, time and space disappear, and only the divine presence exists.

Meditation is, in its essence, simply a process that enables the divine consciousness to express itself through man; it is the appeasement of every movement of the being and the mind, that with its movement creates the illusion within itself that it is something else, that there is something else, and not the divine consciousness.

THE BENEFITS OF MEDITATION IN EVERYDAY LIFE

It would be wrong to conclude that meditation refers only to higher and ultimate goals. All realities are in parallel in the holographic universe, everything is interconnected. That's why the effects and benefits of meditation are valuable in all areas of life. And if it resolves the fundamental existential question, you can imagine how successfully it resolves all those less important ones!

The practice of meditation has already been scientifically proven as the most effective tool in the field of psychotherapy, helping people with the most difficult psychological disorders, like schizophrenia, to less critical issues, such as neuroses and depression; it also aids therapy for dealing with human relationships. All mental disorders are the direct consequence of a lack of objective awareness and the ability to understand the functioning of the mind itself. There is no method which brings better understanding of the mind than meditation. Every successful psychotherapy treatment is based on the cessation of identification with the contents of the mind, with traumas from the past and convictions that are unfounded in reality. With correct meditation, with the cessation of identification with contents of the mind, and with finding a stronghold in one reality, people with any experiences and any possible contents of the mind can find relief.

Meditation is extremely helpful in learning too. The experimental implementation of meditation in schools has yielded excellent results. Also, the same is true in hospitals treating organic diseases.

Meditation is a direct method of awakening the whole body and mind. It is not necessary to do anything else with consciousness, as it solves all misunderstandings by itself. Everything falls into place naturally with meditation.

The basic effect of meditation harmonizes the human being with his essence and the environment.

Such unison is the basic condition for organizing a normal human society in the future.

Such unison of the human being itself will bring forth a normal human society.

THE PHYSICS OF CONSCIOUSNESS IN MEDITATION

If we observe what happens in meditation from the point of view of the frequencies of existence, or more accurately their existence as energy and consciousness, we arrive at the conclusion that meditation is a transition from the Hertzian frequency to the non-Hertzian.

The manifested world of rough 'material' shapes comprise the Hertzian frequencies of energy. Its unmanifested aspect, the universal quantum field, consists of non-Hertzian frequencies. Consciousness reflects their difference, using the mechanism of the mind. ***The mind stands exactly between the non-Hertzian frequency of the quantum field and the unmanifested divine consciousness, and the Hertzian frequency of the manifested world; the mind originates as the contrast of these two frequencies.*** They have to refract somewhere. The point of their refraction is what is known to us as the mind. This is why the mind is able to reflect both frequencies - the manifested world and the unmanifested, body and soul, 'this' world and otherworldly contents. The mind reflects everything. For this reason, the mind opts to behave like an entity, an ego, although it actually does not exist - or exists only as an illusion that once we start searching for, we cannot find. All of Buddhist teaching speaks of this when analyzing the basic blank nature of all phenomena, of the non-existence of the mind or any solid subject tied to the mind. This partly is true, but it's also true that that mind exists, because if it were not real we would not be aware of it. The mind is merely a contrast which spontaneously emerges between two essential areas of existence, the unmanifested non-Hertzian and the manifested Hertzian. This reveals the secret of how a mind can exist, even though it is nowhere to be found. It exists only as a contrast, not as an entity - like a shadow.

If we view the source of the divine consciousnesses or non-Hertzian quantum field, *akasha*, as light, and the Hertzian field as some form of a rough physical shape, then the shadow which is created by the contrast of light and shape can provide us with a clearer picture of what a mind truly is. The mind is like that shadow. If there were no shadow, we would not be able to distinguish between the shape and the light. All the differentiation of consciousness and understanding is based on that distinction between the light and the shape, which the shadow makes possible. This shadow is the mind. This is why the mind is a mechanism that tells us the difference between the Absolute and the relative, the non-Hertzian and the Hertzian, the spiritual and the material. The mind is only a place where the conscious is able to differentiate between a myriad of frequencies.

However, due to the holographic nature of reality, in which nothing is separate and everything is interconnected, that which distinguishes is also what connects. It must be one and the same mechanism that differentiates and connects. That is the mind. The mind simultaneously differentiates and connects, awakens and leads to delusions, simply because it stands exactly between the Hertzian and the non-Hertzian frequencies of reality, as their contrast and their point of contact, which is also their point of their distinction - the distinction whose only purpose is recognition of the unity of the divine consciousness in all frequencies and in all expressions.[5] This

---

[5] The mind is composed of the whole being of man, of seven psychoenergetic centres or chakras. All chakras represent the scope of

is how the mind disappears: when it reaches its limits and recognizes that nothing but the divine consciousness exists, and that the mind is only its reflection, it's gone. Then there is no duality, no contrast, no contradiction which can be created by the mind.

The key role of the mind in connecting unmanifested and manifested phenomena can best be described as creative. The simple connection of the non-Hertzian and Hertzian frequencies and the manifested and unmanifested cosmos is not enough; it is necessary for this merging point to be expressed as creativity. Only through creativity can the superiority and unity of the transcendental divine consciousness in all its aspects and frequencies be displayed. This creativity is described in esoteric philosophy as the divine mind, Nous or Logos. The mind of an average man is just a much paler and smaller shadow of the original shadow, but it's still powerful enough to be the deciding factor in determining which frequencies will be manifested from the overall unmanifested basis of everything. This is precisely what the mind keeps doing, all the time: *it focuses the manifestation of certain non-Hertzian frequencies*. These frequencies then become more complex, up until the point they are materialized in their ultimate Hertzian form. In other words, this is how ideas are realized, this is the way in which a thought becomes a word, a deed, object or phenomenon is created. The creative power of the mind lies in this: it focuses certain frequencies from the universal

---

frequencies that range from the completely non-Hertzian, in the highest chakra (sahasrara), to the lowest chakra (muladhara), which is completely Hertzian. For more details on how consciousness and existence merge and refract through man, through chakras, through various states of consciousness, energy and the mind, see my book "Samadhi - The Unity of Consciousness and Existence."

non-Hertzian quantum field, to which it assigns the form of ideas or thoughts (this is why the mind is no different from thought), which then descend to lower dimensions until they get materialized. What is created in this manner is always new, as originality is the essence of creativity, but also makes sense, is novel in a way which expresses and discovers the deeper meaning of events, which manifest the unmanifested invariably in an original way - because at the base of the unmanifested is the divine consciousness, and the nature of consciousness is transcendental, timeless, which means that its every reflection must always be original. Repetition and imitation are the opposites of consciousness. This is why there is nothing identical in the entire manifested cosmos.

This is also why there is a function in the mind to connect and separate divine frequencies; it simultaneously has a creative function and a limiting function; it slows down and restricts the spontaneous manifestation of everything, all non-Hertzian frequencies, by performing constant repetitions and imitations. It itself is conditioned by thought and patterns of action. However, this is simultaneously a creative function, because if the unmanifested contents were to manifest without due control, without the option of limiting and slowing the functioning of the mind, then nothing new would emerge, there would be no differences. This means the manifestation of the cosmos would not be a possibility. This is why there is nothing negative or wrong in all of existence. Wrong is an impossibility.

The conflict and contradiction of these two functions of the mind give rise to crystallization of a higher transcendental consciousness in the mind, and that is why it can only be expressed in the mind.

This definition of the mind is presented here, for the first time ever. The correct practice of meditation will help you understand it completely, because meditation is nothing but the ability to understand the true nature of the mind, all the way through; that is, to the point of its completion. It is not possible to understand the true nature of the mind and for the mind to perpetuate, to survive. The mind is like a boat which only serves one purpose: taking us across the river, over to the other side. We do not carry the boat with us beyond that point.

If there are two frequencies, then there has to be a common ground which enables them both. Since the mind is the contrast of two frequencies, it has the ability to reflect both completely; and once it manages to reflect them completely, it automatically finds the common denominator, their joint background, which is one divine consciousness of the soul, which is everything. When all contrasts disappear in this way, the mind also disappears, and only the divine consciousness remains - which is no different from existence itself. Existence then does not need any further design by the mind. Design is left lying in the shadow, in the darkness of ignorance.

When in meditation we calm our entire being, and our mind too, then we transform it to a non-Hertzian state; the entire Hertzian field disappears and only the original state of the divine consciousness of the Absolute remains, which has non-Hertzian properties. That's why in meditation the objective world disappears, because Hertzian frequencies disappear. The calmness found in meditation is actually the cessation of the Hertzian state of our being. To be more precise, since it is not possible to annul one at the expense of the other, we harmonize these two frequencies; we align and harmonize them with a calming that is actually us growing in the understanding that they are one and the same frequency of one 'divine particle'; the contrast between them disappears and the mind in meditation also disappears.

MISTAKES IN MEDITATION

Meditation is the act of connecting the mind with consciousness of the soul. The consciousness of our soul is our connection to the source of existence, our connection to the divine Absolute.

This fact about meditation is expressed in two ways: firstly, consciousness of the soul is the most powerful pull a man can experience in this world, a pull always in operation, even when man is unaware of it; and secondly, the nature of that pull makes it work in parallel realities - it acts in all possible ways, and it is always available to us.

When a man in meditation experiences pure consciousness for the first time - that is, consciousness which has been purified for long enough from the illusions of the bodily mind/ego - and manages to connect it to his higher mind, and by doing so with consciousness of the soul, although it only lasts for a brief moment, it is enough to leave an indelible mark. This, in turn, creates an enormous attraction. Many people are changed by such an experience, for the better and for good; it inspires them to devote more effort to meditation, and they further become convinced it is the right path. However, if that first powerful impression is misunderstood as final cognition, and if it gets confused with pre-existing patterns of the mind, or if one does not continue the regular discipline of meditation to deepen understanding, then there is a risk for the mind to turn that first impression into its last, for the mind to turn it into some religion or an obsession.

Becoming aware of the higher state of mind or consciousness of the soul must be followed with the objective knowledge and understanding of what that actually means, the order of things in existence, why everything happens and in what context.

The answers to all these questions are given in the science of *Sânkhya*, which details all the categories of existence (*prakrti*) and their relation to consciousness of the soul (*purusha*).[6] The knowledge of this is necessary to every meditant.

However, the science of sânkhya is not well-known, because it is completely objective and accurate, and this world is dominated by illusions. This is why people are prone to accepting many misconceptions in an effort to understand life.

Apart from the objective knowledge given by the science of sânkhya, meditation is practiced with the everyday strengthening of attention and insight into the true nature of events, which in Buddhism is called vipassana and satipatthâna.

Once an individual surpasses the limitations of the mind, he/she is exposed to the higher states of consciousness; this can get out of control and wreak havoc on people's lives. Higher consciousness gives insights that have a great power to attract, but without the proper understanding and context they can only increase confusion. Many people are able to experience contact with higher consciousness without meditation, using drugs or sometimes just spontaneously, when some prior event blocks the brain from slowing perception - an event such as clinical death, for example. Then, suddenly, the doors

---

[6] For everything on the science of Sânkhya see my book "Sânkhya – The Ancient Science of Nature and Human Soul."

of perception of higher consciousness and the mind are overflowed with insights that one cannot understand, all of which are new but have enormous energy and inviting lure. Such man can see higher dimensions, the beings that inhabit them, and he can see the causes of events that are invisible to the physical mind. This is often too much for the mind and thus can lead to some mental disorders. The problem is that the mind kept its old structure as it was exposed to a higher consciousness with no structure, and which is all-pervading.

The solution to this problem is in parallel work on the knowledge and on the being, as Gurdjieff said; getting oneself acquainted with knowledge of nature and existence, hand-in-hand with the practice of meditative delving. The solution is in regular meditation, with which initial experiences of a higher state of consciousness will be strengthened and prolonged, and in acquiring objective knowledge on the context in which all states of consciousness can be found, which is the knowledge of sânkhya.

The parallel work on the knowledge and the being is essentially the act of raising the level of awareness of all the dimensions of existence, that, at the same time, constitute our being. This is why this type of meditation is recommended here, the type that works with all the dimensions of the being, thus rendering awareness of the body, feelings, the will and the mind of an individual being. *All confusion in meditation, and awareness in general, occur when the meditant works in only one dimension and neglects the others, when too much emphasis is put on one at the expense of the others.* For example, when only the discipline of the body and the physical mind (ethics), or only the mind itself (mantras, prayers), or only feelings and religious devotion (bhakti) are in focus. Fanaticism and exclusivity are always necessary to maintain such unnatural one-sidedness. This is the rule of thumb with all religious sects.

It is necessary to work cohesively with all the aspects of the human being, in parallel, and give them equal amounts of attention, in order to understand them completely. Actually, all of human ignorance occurs only because of this division between consciousness and a lack of unity of the entire being. Such a man is always in confusion and imbalance. One who raises the level of awareness harmoniously, throughout all the dimensions of his being, always looks perfectly harmonious and well-balanced. Early Buddhists described such a meditant as 'his movements are so perfect and smooth like the flowing oil'.

No trip to higher states of consciousness is of use if we fail to understand the nature and context of those higher states, the nature of existence, if we lack objective knowledge about existence, and why things happen the way they happen. Of course, this insight is possible only a higher consciousness, and the consciousness brings it along all by itself; but it has to be adapted to the mind and its cognitive abilities. If that understanding does not adjust itself to the mind and the practical life of the body, then it is not worth much. It may even be counterproductive. That higher consciousness and divine reality always exist outside the mind, but as an abstract force of the divine Absolute. All problems and tasks of meditation boil down to adapting enough for the abstract divine force to conform the mind to reality, and not for the mind to simply disappear in a collision with reality.

When the mind conforms with divine reality, then the divine reality acts through man with its creativity. This is at the base of the Christian idea that 'God becomes the man' and that man conforms to God. 'Son of God' is not Christ only, but every man who manages to transcend the mind.

If the mind collides with reality and disappears because of its impersonal energy, then man may become either mentally disturbed (especially if he has the misfortune of living in the West), or respected as a 'divine lunatic' (if he lives in the East or among the Sufi community - such as *masti*, 'intoxicated with God', among people who understand what has happened to him). In either case, he cannot act creatively, he is unable to express the divine consciousness rationally, even though he can manifest some 'supernatural' states and powers, though mostly in an impractical way.

Anyone who realizes a higher perception without meditation will lose it over time, because it fades away and changes. This is why such a person tries to retain the original memory of the event through the means of some ritual practice, beliefs or drugs, depending on how he originally came to experience a higher perception.

The true power that the divine consciousness has over a weak mind is best shown to us by religious fanatics who, without so much as thinking, sacrifice their own lives, claiming to do so in the name of the divine consciousness; and the degree of ignorance they possess is clearly shown when they sacrifice other people's lives.

Fundamentalism in all religions is the best example of the power aspiration towards the divine really has, but without any understanding and without the practice of meditation. Wherever meditation is missing, blind ritualism and conditioning through religion exists.

The power of the divine Absolute is impersonal and the mind represents the ability to give it shape, which reflects some of its possibilities. The initial experiences the mind has of the divine presence spontaneously lead to disappearance in it, the loss of personality; its attractive power is huge and difficult to resist. One who suddenly and without sufficient preparation becomes acquainted with the highest reality loses their every connection to this world and life; he becomes 'detached'. Only understanding the true nature of the divine presence, through all the dimensions of existence and through our own being, can help the mind to stay rooted; and this is the understanding that there is nothing outside the divine reality, that it is everything and the mind exists only for the divine consciousness to be able to express itself creatively, in all possible ways. This is why it is not necessary to disappear and nullify ourselves and our mind when surrendering to the divine reality. *Our soul was not born here in the body just to escape at the first opportunity.* Human beings and minds exist so that the divine reality, through our souls, can express itself in as much detail and as creatively as possible, to become aware through all the dimensions of existence and all experiences. *We came here to connect all possibilities of existence to the divine consciousness, to creatively express the divine consciousness which enables nature. In other words, to give meaning to existence*. Certainly, it invariably exists, even without us, but if it is not aware, then it is not actualized. The meaning of existence is in actualization of meaning through awareness. By annulling anything, we annul the meaning of existence. With our awareness, we must participate in existence, and not turn our back or run away from it.

  There are two types of awakening: sudden and gradual. The sudden can happen to anybody, but is quickly lost. It stays only in the memory. Zen Buddhism is based on nourishing the consciousness after a sudden awakening, which is always possible. But outside the strict discipline of Zen, a sudden awakening is usually dangerous and harmful to man, because he does not understand the meaning of what's happened to him.

Gradual awakening is the cultured understanding of the whole of existence, through working on ourselves. The science of meditation in Patanjali's Yoga Sutras and in early Buddhism is dedicated to this. It is a science that's available to everybody, and which leads man to the highest levels of consciousness - albeit gradually - with the fullest understanding of the entire process and its meaning, through adapting oneself to that reality. There we become the reality that we search for and perceive from the outside world.

Many meditants, and those who spontaneously experienced transcendence of the mind, have lost their life compass in the crash with the higher consciousness. A man really needs to know what he is doing in meditation - his most important work is on himself, even more so, that is more significant than anything else.

This knowledge is always available; when we turn to the divine it automatically turns to us, gives us absolutely everything we need, through events, people and books; the only problem we face is in the readiness and flexibility of the mind to accept them, in its liberation from concepts and patterns to which it had previously been a slave to.

The difficulty this liberation poses comes from the fear which the mind/ego expresses as a defense mechanism when confronting a higher force than itself, which it does not understand. Because of this fear, the mind/ego is able to defend itself and rationalize its survival by any means necessary. Philosophy and religious themes are his favourite weapons in this struggle for survival, as is refusing meditation. It needs to be overcome with the proper understanding of what is really going on.

Many mistakes which occur during meditation are also related to the matter of speed. If we progress too quickly during the practice of meditation, and our capacity for submission is enhanced, we can experience the opening of portals for those insights we are not yet capable of comprehending. Meditation opens the doors of perception to higher dimensions, which can often happen through out-of-body experiences. For this reason it is necessary to have objective knowledge of all the dimensions of nature, of the natural order of reality which is most accurately presented in the science of sânkhya. This is why a very thorough meditation manual, such as Patanjali's *Yoga Sutras*, is based on the science of sânkhya.

Without such objective knowledge about the higher extrasensory dimensions of nature, a man who has quickly gained extrasensory perception could fall into a trap of uncritical and false reasoning, thinking that what he perceives as extrasensory is supernatural, and therefore a priori spiritual and true. Only in the science of sânkhya do we have true information about the higher, extrasensory dimension (astral worlds), and know that are also a part of nature, even though we are unable to perceive them with our senses, even though we enter them via out-of-body experiences. This is far from authentic spirituality and the ultimate goal of awakening. However, these higher dimensions have a strong pull on us and it is easy to become convinced that we discovered 'Kingdom Come', just because we have found ourselves outside of our body, gaining the power of insight - something that the senses do not have.

Natural conditionality is not only material; it includes far more, namely immaterial dimensions, which are in some religions presented as higher worlds (heavenly kingdom' or 'paradise') where celestial beings reside and are falsely presented as the ultimate goal to which we should aspire. The overcoming of the physical world of senses is only the first step in the path of liberation. Many have stumbled on that first step and interpreted their decline back to themselves as having reached the end goal, the revelation.

In reality, all official religions are based on such misguided views; higher dimensions of nature, which still condition man, are presented as the highest divine worlds and the goal of religion. Only Buddhism, which is not a religion and consists only of the practice of meditation, teaches us correctly that the higher worlds are not the ultimate goal, but the final awakening of the human soul from all dimensions of nature that conditions us.

All of this is stated in Patanjali's *Yoga Sutras* when it comes to the removal of subconscious impressions, samskara and vasana, the impressions and patterns which led us through life and all its incarnations. Our subconscious is actually what affects us from those higher, supernatural dimensions of nature. **The higher dimensions of nature are our inner world, our unconscious - because man is a microcosm, made up of all the dimensions of nature.** That is why the impressions which we carry with us outlive the body, and follow us in all incarnations. Meditation serves only to burn them in the fire of consciousness, so they cannot act through the mind; that is, they cannot further shape karma and bind consciousness of the soul to bodily incarnations.

There are various individual obstacles that occur in the beginning of the practice of meditation. Light or sound effects may occur, that attract attention or disturb the process, and which distract the meditant or interfere with meditation. All of these distractions should be discarded, because they fall under the category of disturbances, seductive scenes of different deities, as well as interfering faceless appearances. We should ignore them completely, and they will disappear. They will survive only to the point we decide to give them attention.

Meditation itself increases consciousness and lowers the level of unconsciousness. It is like drying out a lake. As the level of water falls, we bit by bit discover things that were hidden at the bottom of the lake. Similarly with an increase of consciousness and awareness, unconscious contents begin to appear, maybe from this or previous lives. These contents have their own energy and once they are made aware of, their energy is released. All of this has a varying effect on us, depending on the nature of the content. It can work only as a memory, as a vision related to that content. It can affect us as some vague feeling, pleasant or uncomfortable; maybe there is pain, physical or emotional; we may experience a lot of stress or sudden excitement; or see the contents reappearing constantly. All this should be considered only as an obstacle to proper meditation. In meditation, we do not deal with the contents of the mind, but with consciousness itself, with transcendence of all contents - with witnessing and testimony, without ties.

Maybe one of the biggest mistakes regarding meditation is that meditation itself is not necessary; that there are other, more efficient or easier methods. These, most often, relate to the use of psychoactive substances. Their effect, however, is opposite to the effect of meditation. They act in a very subtle way and can create the fatal illusion that meditation is not necessary. But with proper meditation the highest states of consciousness can be achieved, with insight and bliss, which even the best psychoactive substances (like DMT) are not capable of providing; meditation creates a state that is permanent and comprehensive, and takes into consideration the entire life, not just temporary and subjective experiences, as substances do.

The use of psychoactive substances will prevent correct understanding of all the dimensions of our being and existence; they will not bring us the perfection of understanding and function. This is what sets meditants apart from drug users: the former become perfect in functioning, while the latter are distracted; the former become better human beings, and the latter remain the same, with only their convictions changed. In short, substances affect primarily the mind and the state of the mind, while meditation affects the entire being, in all dimensions, inspiring an alternation in lifestyle that introduces an awakening into the light of consciousness of the soul. Substance users rely on substances as an external means for achieving an internal goal, forcing them to become dependent on drugs. A drug addict, with the help of substances, asks to gain understanding. The meditant relies solely on himself and the power of personal change and functioning to achieve understanding, and this process of reaching understanding is the only thing which brings full understanding, both of the body and the mind, of consciousness of the soul, and their interrelations.

One of the most common mistakes in meditation is that a person who has little initial experience of transcendental consciousness and insight, without work on himself or objective knowledge, presumes that he has discovered everything he needs, or at least enough to be a teacher to others, to spread knowledge and to give instruction for meditation - simply because of the great attractive power of higher consciousness which he has discovered. Such people are known for imposing their "spirituality" on everyone. This is a big mistake.

Most people have not come to this world to wake up, but to dream some dream, to live the karmic contents they have inherited, some other topic or program of experiences which is too strong for interruption, and which is needed to mature the consciousness of the soul. If you try to point out the truth to these people and their need for liberation - which they are not in the least bit prepared for, and which they do not want - they might choose to rebel against you with strong agitation, because you are shaking their cage. People who are ready to learn and who are ready for discipline will always search for it on their own and persevere when doing so. That is why spirituality and true knowledge can never be imposed. It is always necessary to be protected from the abuse of people with an inferior level of maturity.

The solution to all mistakes in meditation is found in regular meditation and discipline only, and by avoiding turning it into an obsession; in not confusing the discipline of meditation with religious devotion and philosophizing, or with anything else for that matter. The solution is in discipline of meditation in all dimensions, not only on the mental plane, but also the physical and emotional. This is the practice which we will outline here.

THE NEED FOR A TEACHER IN MEDITATION

This is one of the biggest questions in meditation. You have to learn somewhere and where you learn is very important.

The solution is readily available simply by understanding what meditation actually is - what we talked about at the beginning. It is the connection of consciousness of the lower mind with consciousness of the higher mind and consciousness of the soul. That is achieved through the practice of disciplining the lower mind. This discipline consists of simple calming of the lower mind and the body, so consciousness of the higher mind and soul can manifest through the body and lower mind. While the lower mind is dominant with the body, active and led by its subjective principles and urges, consciousness of the higher mind and soul cannot come to the fore. Therefore, the beginning of meditation is not possible if the lower mind is still in charge. Knowledge about the need for meditation should reach the higher mind and consciousness of the soul. This knowledge has been around for centuries and has passed the test of time, through many practitioners. It has existed since time immemorial, back when people had a much greater connection with consciousness of the soul. This knowledge was systematically written down by Patanjali in the second century BC, and today we know it as Yoga Sutras. However, these are just proof that, in a nutshell, convey much more ancient knowledge, sayings that serve as guidelines and a reminder for the practitioners of meditation. The age and tradition of Yoga Sutras indicate that this work is an authentic source for initiating the practice of meditation.

Although we can find in these sayings everything we need to know for the practice of meditation, the lower mind is an obstacle to understanding all of it immediately. Therefore, man needs support from someone else, who has already gone down this path; he also needs encouragement in the form of an example that proves that this road is the right one, someone who is able to testify with the results of his own meditation. Such people are natural teachers to new meditants. These teachers of meditation did not do anything of their own accord or at their sole discretion. They only, thanks to their own connection with the higher consciousness and consciousness of the soul, establish contact with their disciple's consciousness of the soul, and in doing so make it possible for the consciousness of the soul of the student in question to be influenced, for further practice and training. The best example of this are Sufi teachers.

Therefore, the real teacher in meditation is the consciousness of the soul of the man himself. When he takes a step towards consciousness of the soul as a consequence of his attempt to meditate, or as a result of his maturity which is synchronized with that consciousness, then consciousness of the soul takes a step towards him. The consciousness of the soul functions on the inside and on the outside. On the inside, inspiration plays a key role, and on the outside, consciousness pushes itself towards him. Consciousness of the soul uses different means in order to turn man inward, towards himself; it functions by orchestrating various events, with the participation of other people and through various life experiences, which can be both pleasant and desirable but often very difficult, depending on the degree of stubbornness of the lower mind. That is why, when the consciousness of the soul of the disciple can reach out to the consciousness of the soul of another meditant who has achieved the practice of meditation, then it has an easy job - it can affect the disciple most efficiently through such a well-tuned instrument. Such an instrument is then known as a "meditation teacher". Such a teacher in reality does nothing but consciously take upon himself the role of the higher mind of the disciple, which he is in contact with, and help the higher mind of the disciple like an intermediary or interpreter of the messages intended for the lower mind of the disciple.

Truly, consciousness of the soul is the only teacher. It guides us and teaches us, from the moment we're born and in various ways. Most of these ways we experience as temptations which are as difficult and painful as the lower mind/ego is strong and stubborn.

When we become mature enough for meditation, training is maximally enhanced and it becomes much more detailed and precise. Consciousness of the soul gives us all the necessary information for meditation, which can also be found in this book.

It is enough just to begin the practice of meditation sincerely, imperfect as it may be, and consciousness of the soul will immediately respond more strongly. In order to recognize the teacher within us, we need to see him in everything we do, and observe things from the outside. Consciousness of our teacher, consciousness of the soul, is the same consciousness that enables existence. That is why we need to recognize its action in everything, above all in everything we do and observe. Life itself becomes our teacher of meditation.[7] All temptations are the means of realization of meditation. By becoming a better human being, we become a better meditant.

Such were the teachers in ancient times, but today there are too few teachers of this grandeur. There are more of them, in countries where Buddhism and Zen predominate. Today the teaching of meditation is largely about the practice of mind control, practised by various sects. If it is not a question of direct functioning of a sect, then it is nonetheless the same, albeit hidden through New Age ideology, which acts as a sect but in an informal way, so as to seduce those who are opposed to the idea of sects. It is easy to recognize whether it is real teaching of meditation or sectarian programming, by analyzing the consequences; but also by the many details that give them away. Sectarian is everything that abolishes the free will of an individual, or falsely presents freedom as licentiousness, and being a slave to some authority. Group meditations fall into this category because they manipulate the energy of an individual. All group meditations that are performed at a scheduled time, under the pretext of 'sending positive energy', are actually a theft of energy and programming of the mind. The motive itself is meaningless, because energy is at the base of existence and consciousness, and there is no need to send it somewhere at a certain time; everyone has as much as they need, and as much as they deserve. But that is why it can be stolen from naïve people. There are both physical and non-physical entities living off stolen energy. Some of these entities have also established sects which deal with programming of the mind and stealing energy. Energy theft

---

[7] See a more thorough approach in the work of P. D. Ouspensky: "The Fourth Way."

is most often performed by the awakening of kundalini. Kundalini can be activated with certain methods, but if it is not followed by a mature consciousness and proper insight, it is a destructive force, and man becomes used by different entities. Kundalini is the full potential of energy in man. If it is activated, energy will be given to the contents of the psyche of the man in question. Unfortunately, an unenlightened man has almost nothing good in his psyche. All the nonsense and misconceptions hiding there will get energy and will break out in the harshest way. This is why mental hospitals are full of people who have awakened kundalini prematurely and artificially. A man with an awakened kundalini is a real treat for such entities. They have directly inspired many sects with this aim in mind.

The artificial kundalini activation using some techniques is the most typical and common twisting of the true nature of spirituality carried out by New Age sects. They replaced the cause and consequence. It is promised that if you open perception first and reach insight into higher dimensions (often with the help of drugs) you will be "enlightened," or at least one step closer to it. The truth is the other way round: first you have to become enlightened, awakened, to open your perception to the higher dimensions, to objective reality. How will you be able to understand anything from that higher, objective reality, if you remain unawakened and subjective? The real awakening of kundalini follows the true awakening of consciousness of the soul in man. The consciousness itself awakens and raises kundalini, because the consciousness is at the base of energy. Energy without consciousness is a destructive force.

The next common characteristic of swindlers is charging for their services. The only price which man should pay on the spiritual path is his own effort and work on himself. Everything else is theft.

However, all this is a part of the temptation of consciousness and the process of maturing. Naive, lazy and immature people should pay the false gurus to satisfy their need for easy and false goals; they will learn from their mistakes. Everyone gets what they deserve. This is all energy economizing. It cannot be static; if we do not use it, somebody else will use it for/on us. If we are not our own masters, somebody else will impose their will on us. Our unconscious is revealed to us in this way; all those entities and fake gurus that keep stealing our energy and leading us to delusions, point a finger in the direction of the unconscious part of us, they show us what we are not aware of, they reveal and materialize our unconscious contents, and in that way they help us become more conscious.

Consciousness of our soul as our teacher uses all of this, being both the teacher of meditation and life, as well.

MEDITATION AND DEATH
SIMILARITIES AND DIFFERENCES

In the beginning we said that meditation or contemplation is a method which awakens man in understanding reality, using an accelerated method; or to be more precise, a method with which the illusion of time is removed, the illusion during which we imagine that we are something else and not what we truly are, that we are separated from the highest reality. With meditation, man attunes himself to reality. Harmonization with reality is the teaching and practice of meditation.

This is based on the fact that the highest reality goes far beyond one individual human life.

This is why the essence of meditation - harmonization with reality - is based on the fact that man does not begin to exist with physical birth, nor is his existence limited to the physical body. This implies that the context, the reason for meditation to exist, includes the periods before birth and after death. If a man is created at birth and disappears with death, meditation would be completely impossible and unnecessary because there would be nothing that overcomes physical life. The fact remains that there could not be a physical life, were it not for everything that surpasses it. The invisible spiritual part which goes far beyond is much bigger and more powerful, so much so that all physical existence looks like a pale shadow in comparison to it.

Since reality goes far beyond the physical world, meditation is a method with which man becomes fully realized and present in existence, truly unconditioned and authentically his (own) in all dimensions, not only in this physical reality. Only with meditation does man begin to exist truly, more accurately, than with his mind which is limited to the physical body; he discovers his true existence. The higher dimensions are those in which man exists before physical birth and after death. This means that man starts to exist truly only when he overcomes the illusion of death and all the illusions of life, the illusions that he is only a body and mind; when his mind that's identified with the body (the ego) dies. In other words, from our point of view, from the physical mind and ego we are using now, we really begin to exist only when we disappear. From this point of view even meditation appears as a process of disappearance of an individual. This bears great resemblance to dying. Viewed from 'below', from the point of view of the mind and ego, meditation is like dying alive, and viewed from 'above', from the point of view of the transcendental human soul, which is the reflection of the divine reality, it is a big awakening and the return of man to his authentic state, which he has before and after the process of incarnations, before birth and after the death of the body.

In this way, meditation includes the death of man and is very closely associated with it. In fact, the greater part of the experience of meditation is related to understanding and experiencing death; life is only the basis for this experience.

The similarity between meditation and death is nothing but the experience or awakening to the wider dimension of our existence, which we had had before we were born and which we will have after death of the physical body.

This is the key requirement for cognition of reality: overcoming the physical limitations that we have in the body and mind.

All of meditation boils down to overcoming psychophysical limitations, surpassing the body and mind. All of the discipline which leads us to meditation is about awakening and retraining the body and mind.

We can see that life itself teaches us exactly this all our life we learn how to overcome the body and mind. From the stories of Scheherazade, across all cultures, religions, science and creativity, there is one common focus: overcoming death and transience, and all the limitations of body and mind, together with ascertaining knowledge of what transcends us.

This fact is so clear and has such a potent effect on all those who aspire toward spirituality that some individuals, especially those in early stages and still immature, can experience the higher divine reality, its values and the most supreme truth, as a call for death or sacrifice of life (one's own or other people's).

When the illusions of life are overcome in a spontaneous, unconscious and traumatic manner, the issue of suicide becomes quite real. Each suicidal man, who stepped over the edge of the abyss spontaneously, came to the experience of overcoming all the illusions of life, to which meditants come in samadhi. Each meditant, in order to come to samadhi, has to have the same determination as a man about to commit suicide, on the verge of death. He must have the experience of complete separation from his entire life.

In fact, in order for a man to be mature enough for meditation, he has to have such separation. Similar to an artist who cannot create genuine works of art if he has to paint on commission, who only experiences true creativity when his need to do so is bigger than life, and he cannot do anything else; we only sit in meditation when we are in the mood or when we have time. Quite the opposite: in real meditation we sit only when we do not have time for anything else, when we cannot do anything else, when our life up until that moment is finished, for good.

Only with the discipline of meditation can one come to the insight that suicide is absolutely the worst thing to do; it is the confirmation of identification with the body and mind, which is directly opposed to the principle of meditation. In meditation, when everything becomes clear, when body and mind do not exist, do we see that they have never been our true characteristic; the issue has always been in our identification as an expression of the unconscious, and the cessation of identification as an awakening. This is the true victory over body and mind, and of all life's drama, temptation and distress. In a real awakening, we see that it has never been about the body and the mind, not even about life itself in the body, and even less about any life drama we experienced in the body and mind.

All of the suffering which leads us to suicide gets its meaning and purpose when it brings us to the maturity needed for meditation, to the insight that the attitude of consciousness towards itself is the real problem, and the attitude toward life itself. Therefore, the attitude towards meditation is exactly the same as the attitude towards the meaning of life. Meditation comes with maturity, with knowing that we should resolve everything in our inner world, in our relation towards existence, and not just on the outside. Existence has always been perfect, because it cannot be otherwise. We need to be (in ourselves) the reality towards which we strive on the outside. In the ultimate reality, the internal and external are one and same.

More specifically, when we are identified with the mind, then we are primarily identified with the body.

However, the identification with the mind is much more subtle and deeper, and from it we liberate ourselves with more difficulty. Identification with the mind is the cause of our every effort to set ourselves free of the body, and of life. The mind will always blame the body first and then all outer life; if necessary it will kill itself and anyone else, for the purpose of self-preservation. The mind always projects all of its contents outwards. ***The mind itself is nothing but the projection of consciousness outward, into space and time.*** In that way, only because of identification with the mind, space and time, man gets the idea that the body should be killed - his own or someone else's - in order for him to solve some problem, some physical limitation, to reach what is above body and mind. Time is the only death which exists. Only when we overcome the mind and time in meditation, can we see that the body never existed as our body, that it is a timeless presence, an inseparable part of the whole of nature, of the divine Absolute.

      Together with the conscious overcoming of identification with the body and the mind, there has always been the idea of resurrection, globally present from time immemorial, as the backbone of all real spirituality in man. However, resurrection rests on identification with the body and mind; it is the outer projection of identification with the body and mind, which occurs due to a misunderstanding of the true meaning of meditation and the lack of its practice; and consequently, we believe really need to experience death, in order to know 'God' - though remaining alive during the process. In each real meditation, man dies and resurrects. Each meditant is 'The Son of God' because he comes to the point where he recognizes that we all came from the same divine source.

From the inner conscious experience of overcoming identification with the body and the mind in meditation, the religion of resurrection is projected outward, with Christianity and its 'Son of God' in the leading role. Equally, it could be said that all of this staging is projected to deceive people, rather than inspire them to search for resurrection in themselves; to sustain them in a perpetual illusion of time through a ritual – in the same way it could be said that the idea of an external resurrection of the 'Son of God' is a reminder of the soul of each man, what he should actually do with himself.

Identification with body and mind is the only death a person should experience in this world. It is also the only experience of death he can experience. The only death that really exists is what our soul experiences when it is born in the body. There is no other death relating to the body and mind, because the body and mind do not exist of their own accord, independently; they are only a reflection of the divine consciousness, which is everything-that-is. The body and mind have never been a part of man and therefore losing them is not an option; in the same way, man cannot keep them forever.

All of physical life is like a mirror for the consciousness of the soul. But that mirror not only reflects reality perfectly, but it also gives a reverse picture of reality: our internal essence, consciousness of the divine soul, appears in that mirror, in the physical world, as opposites - as the external world and life. If we saw in the external world just the reverse reflection of consciousness of the divine soul, it would be ideal, just one step away from divine self-knowledge or enlightenment; but that reflection is so realistic that we actually lose consciousness of ourselves in it and experience it as the rough material world in which we are lost and alienated from ourselves and the divine presence. We enter that mirror where everything is weird, like in a dream. That projection of the divine consciousness into its own reflection exists so we can experience our essence with all available detail, objectively, to poke about at it like small children. The ultimate consequence of consciousness of itself, which we gain through the mirror of the mind and external existence, is a twisting of reality; it appears that we are born in that world and merely exist in it, though that is opposite. We are now, in this physical world, as dead as we can be. The birth of the physical body is our only experience of dying; the death of the body is the awakening of the soul. According to Sufi mystic Mawlana Jalal-ad-Din Rumi: "This world is a dream. Only a sleeper considers it real. Then death comes like dawn, and you wake up laughing at what you thought was your grief."

The one who achieves the goal of meditation, samadhi, or awakening, will laugh for the same reason, here in this life, and much more joyfully.

All of physical life is actually a relationship with death. This can be seen because the peak of meaning of life is reached only in relation to death, and the sacrifice of one's life for an ideal which transcends us. Everything we do in life is in relation to death; we fight for our life in all sorts of ways: we create offspring, new things and forms of existence, new possibilities; we constantly fight for the light of knowledge and understanding in the face of darkness of ignorance and oblivion. Each cognition makes us aware of the wider context, of what goes beyond it, enabling it at the same time, and the widest context of everything, the meaning of life, is what overcomes life itself. Every life is the life of a warrior who dedicates himself to a higher cause and an ideal that transcends him, more or less successfully and manifesting more or less dignity during the struggle. The Samurai, who leaves his life before the battle begins, ensures the total success of the fight; this is the purest expression of the awareness of death and overcoming of the physical body and life. Every real warrior wants to have "a good death," worth living, more than anything else. Anyone who was reborn and experienced a "revelation" had to go through death, in order to "be born in a new life" he had to "die in the old life". All traditional initiations that enable a young and immature person to qualify for a new mature life include the experience of death and rebirth.

In fact, it looks as if the wars in this world exist as the ultimate expression, the catharsis of that battle for life which we constantly strive towards, in all ways, at home, at work, in society, with other people, and mostly with oneself. The meaning of all of these struggles is to crystallize the consciousness of our soul, that has never been encompassed in this body and this life, but goes far beyond it. All of these are, it could be said, empirical ways to awaken the soul.

When we do not have the practice of meditation, then it seems to us that we really need to fight to experience physical death, in order to overcome the conditionality and ignorance of the true nature of the body and mind (resurrection).

Only with the correct practice of meditation can we recognize that reality transcends the body and mind without their sacrifice, directly, without agonizing in suffering; we recognize that the physical reality is not an obstacle to realization of the highest divine reality; that the highest divine reality is omnipresent, much like physical reality itself; that physical reality is actually the most concrete and closest to divine reality that we can experience. Only with the practice of proper meditation can we remove ignorance and see that only the divine reality exists, and that nothing other than that can exist in any way, that our physical separation from the divine reality has never been an option, and therefore we have never been born, nor can we ever die. Meditation is the only proper dying, the only proper awareness of consciousness of the soul. Everything else is torture, through difficult indirect methods, leading to the same goal. That is why meditation is in opposition to struggle and any kind of action.

Speaking in terms of physics, the entire manifested physical world is composed of Hertzian frequencies, its unmanifested aspect, while the universal quantum field is made up of non-Hertzian frequencies. Reality is constructed of both, it is everything-that-it-is and everything-that-can-be. Our mind is a factor that distinguishes between these two frequencies; it itself is actually only a consequence that arises at the point of breaking of these two frequencies. We, as a being that is a mirror image of the microcosm, composed of all the dimensions of nature, experience both frequencies, manifested Hertzian and unmanifested non-Hertzian. ***When the mind is unaware of its true nature, it separates them. When it is conscious, it understands them and recognizes them as a whole.*** The unmanifested non-Hertzian frequency is the source of consciousness and spirit within us, and the manifested Hertzian is the source of the physical body, with all its limitations defined by space and time, together with the mind/ego which uses the unmanifested potential of consciousness within the limits of the body and sensory perception. That is why, for the mind, every experience of transcendence is equal to the experience of death, because it always has to disappear (more precisely: its Hertzian frequencies do) so that the non-Hertzian field of the universal consciousness opens up. Hence, **on this difference of frequencies rests all experiences of death for man,** including physical death.

The experience of death is only a psychological impression that arises from the change in frequency of consciousness from the Hertzian to the non-Hertzian. The experience of birth is also just a psychological impression resulting from a change in the frequency of consciousness from non-Hertzian to Hertzian.

Meditation is the practice of a systematic and well-controlled transition from the Hertzian to the non-Hertzian frequencies of existence, and their harmonization with general reality in human experience. That is why the knowledge that comes with meditation is, in all likelihood, equal to the experience of death people go through in this world - the complete overcoming of an individual life and all attachment to its contents. But this is also why it is the method of healing man's life in the universal, divine reality, because in meditation, in a well-controlled and conscious manner, it happens spontaneously to our souls; they move from a physical to a non-physical world, from the Hertzian to the non-Hertzian field of existence. All our incarnations, all our karma and actions, in this world and in the other world, are only a spontaneous alternation of non-Hertzian and Hertzian frequencies, the interaction between consciousness and existence, spirit and matter. **Meditation is a conscious experimental experience of the entire process, but on a small scale. Because it is conscious, the experience of meditation ends the unconscious rotation of that process, ending karma and transformation, uniting the divine reality in one timeless presence, the way it itself is.** In fact, it doesn't unite only itself, because it is what it always is and cannot be anything else. It unites the microcosm of the human being with existence, to be complete and in harmony with the divine reality, and with all its frequencies.

To put it in a nutshell, meditation and death are similar in all things except one: after the fulfillment of the goal of meditation (*sahaja samadhi*), man continues to live as if nothing has happened. Like he was not even born.

Such a man is called in *advaita vedanta*, *jivan mukta*, which represents a soul which has come to know its real nature during its physical life.

PART TWO

THE PRACTICE OF MEDITATION

The practice of meditation, which will be presented here, is based on the texts from Patanjali's *Yoga Sutras*, (YS), Buddha's *The Great Discourse on the Establishing of Awareness (Mahasatipatthâna sutta)* and *The Shorter Discourses on Voidness (Culasunnata sutta*, M. 121); instructions for sitting in zen meditation by Jasutani-roshi (Haku'un Yasutani, 1885-1973) and my personal experience of meditation during the past 40 years.

GENERAL AND SPECIFIC PREREQUISITES FOR MEDITATION

Meditation is based on three principles and eight conditions.

The first principle is that when the mind is calm, defective views disappear all by themselves. All illusions disperse once we reach a state of calmness. Since all activities originate from the oblivion of the reality of the divine Absolute, starting from the mind and onward all the way to the entire cosmos. In this way, our original, timeless, absolute nature reveals itself to itself. Any other attempt to remove illusions or reach our true nature is always the activity of our mind and ego. The conclusion is that we only go round in circles, along the path line of the contents of our mind.

The first principle is stated at the beginning of Yoga Sutras:

I,2: Yoga is in the cessation of the [blurred particulars] »twists in consciousness« (*cittavrtti*).

I,3: [Only] then [in that cessation of particular twists] »the one who sees« (*drastr*) is in accordance with his true nature (*svarupa*).

I,4: Otherwise [»Man«] is identified with [particular] twists (*vrtti*) [of his own consciousness, mind].

In short, only with calmness, with the cessation of the activities of the mind, can consciousness of the soul in man show its real nature. Always, when identified with activities of the mind, man is unaware of his real nature, of the consciousness of the soul.

The second principle is that we are already the highest Divine reality, which through our minds we try to become or at least realize. The mind continually creates the illusion that we are not, that we are separated. That is why all that's needed is to be calm, and with your calmness to calm down your mind. Here and now. That is why meditation is about awakening, not about the objective achievement of some state which we did not previously have.

The third principle is related to ethics. In order to overcome the mind with calmness, we firstly need our body to be calm; and in order for our body to be calm, our behavior must not be destructive. Therefore, we speak about true calmness of the whole being, and not some partial, temporary and forced calmness, or stiffness. The calmness in meditation is the opposite of stiffness, it is complete serene submission, reconciliation with all of existence, with our whole life. Only with that reconciliation can we achieve independence from everything - the independence which is meditation itself. In order to bring ourselves to such a calm state, to come to terms with existence, it is necessary to have a proper and righteous life, a peaceful conscience. Any turmoil of the being is based on an incorrect lifestyle and unconscious reactions, on misunderstanding and attachment. Correctness in life is achieved through the ethical principles that are outlined as *yama* and *niyama* in Patanjali's Yoga Sutras and *Sila*, Noble Eightfold Path in Buddhism. Without a clean and righteous life there is no tranquility. And without calmness, there is no awakening.

Patanjali's Yoga, which is the source of Buddhist meditation, has eight parts:

Y.S. II, 29: [General] Rules [of good conduct] (*yama*), [specific yogic] obligations (*nyama*), [yogic] sitting position (*asana*), breath control (*pranayama*), restraint of [senses] (*pratyahara*), attention focus (*dharana*), contemplation (*dhyana*) and mindfulness of [being] (samadhi) represent eight members of [yoga].

Yama represents the regulation of correct and healthy relationships with other people and the world around them; the most important qualities are non-violence and unconditional love.

Y.S. II, 30: Abstaining from violence (*ahimsa*), truthfulness (*satya*), refraining from other people's possessions (*asteya*), control of one's own sensuality (*brahmacarya*), giving up on material goods [all things that are not necessary] (*aparigraha*) represent [general] rules of [correct behavior] (*yama*).

Only then is *niyama* possible, regulating a correct and healthy relationship with yourself, an honest life with a clear conscience, a well-disciplined and healthy life.

Y.S. II, 32: Hygiene, contentment [possession of the necessary material goods] (*samtosha*), asceticism (*tapas*), the thoughtful acceptance of the message of the traditional texts and formulas (*svadhyaya*), commitment to Sublime represent [specific yogic] obligations.

Asceticism here means the crystallization of consciousness in challenges, for the sake of becoming aware of one's real needs and rejecting false ones. With starvation we become aware of everything that is excessive in diet; by exposing ourselves to extreme conditions of life, we lose the pleasure of living with modern conveniences, which means the body and ego get rejected; by refraining from speech, one becomes aware of the true meaning of words; having exposed oneself to pain, the body experiences and masters it; and so forth. Asceticism always serves the purpose of awakening, and in true spirituality (the way it is set up in Patanjali's Yoga and Buddhism) must never jeopardize the body and the mind, or become the final goal unto itself.

Only then is **asana** possible - calmness of the body, regulation of the relationship with the body, and the correct position for meditation.

In order for the body to be able to sit for a long time in a position for meditation, it needs to be healthy and slim. That is why old practitioners of meditation developed physical exercises, *hatha yoga*, mostly exercises of stretching, with which the body is filled with energy and with which it is kept in good health. *Hatha yoga* is only an auxiliary part of meditative practice which enables the physical conditions for meditation.

Sitting in meditation or asana involves not only the position of the body, but also the location - the surroundings. In the beginning, the place to meditate needs to be constant, some room in which nobody will disturb you. A closed room is always a better option than an outdoor space, in nature, because in the privacy of our room we will have fewer opportunities to be distracted, by noise, small insects or other people. With growth of experience we can start to meditate anywhere, and then any asana which detaches us from the mind is the right one. It is also better to meditate alone rather than in a group, because the group may mimic one another unconsciously. On the other hand, meditation in a group can help beginners to acquire discipline. Work in a group is necessary and only makes sense for this reason: attaining the much needed discipline for meditation. When more people join in, all working for the same goal, then they can correct each other. That is the whole point of coenobitic monasticism. When a man works alone, he can deceive himself more easily that he is doing something, even if he is off track; he justifies it to himself in a number of ways. Once the discipline is acquired, group work is no longer necessary and can only lead to imitation or acceptance of some collective pattern of living. There are also collective deceptions, not just individual ones.

Finally, asana is calmness of the body, and there is no calmness of the body without a clear conscience and a proper life, to which are dedicated all these preconditions for meditation. Calmness is the opposite of disturbance, and all disturbance is the reflection of an unclear conscience, conflict and imbalance, which represents capsizing from the real state. Meditation is a return to your real authentic state. Therefore, it represents calmness.

Agitation has a Hertzian frequency, while calmness is non-Hertzian.

Only then is **pranayama** possible - regulating your life energy, because calmness of the mind and breath, awareness of energetic activity, goes both ways; without their correctness, meditation is impossible.

Pranayama is the regulation of life energy, *prana*, and it is attained with breathing exercises, which are dealt with in *hatha yoga*, but also with other forms of energy input into the body, such as nutrition. Nutrition represents a rough form of energy input to the body; the finest form is the direct input of air and sun absorbed by chlorophyll, the process which corresponds with hemoglobin (blood) in people, which acts in the same way as chlorophyll does except for one element (iron instead of magnesium). Lungs produce all the protein the organism requires from air, sunlight and the through skin and eyes, reaching hemoglobin and producing the remainder of the body's needs (which is solar yoga). The only form of rough nutrition preferred for meditants is plant-based nutrition (vegan food). All other types of nutrition, based on processed foods, are considered to be a rougher form of nutrition, which, in turn, causes the mind to become rougher. The quality of food determines the quality of the mind. The finer the food is, the finer the mind is, more conscious. Therefore, it has always been a rule that awareness of the mind and liberation from the rough states and identifications directly depends on the light dietary regimen; an even better way is going hungry or fasting.

Only then is *pratyahara* possible - the first turning toward the inner Self and the realization of the need for independence from the outside world, an objective relationship towards all sensual objects; these are the first moments of turning away from the empirical mind towards the higher mind and consciousness of the soul.

The clearer consciousness of the soul is to us, the clearer the danger of letting go to our senses is. That clarity is *pratyahara*. The meditant, according to Buddha's words, **never goes beyond the threshold of his senses. He does so by making himself aware of all the sensory perception that there is, that of the sight, hearing, touch, smell and taste, only the way it is, and nothing else.** He neither attaches to it, nor rejects it. He neither denies it, nor does he block or judge any sensory experience; on the contrary, he becomes aware of each experience for what it is, without attaching to it, projecting it, without any associations. If he denied or judged anything in connection with sensory experiences, then he would not be objectively conscious and independent from them. Independence from sensory experiences can be reached only with objective awareness, not with rejection.

With *pratyahara*, for the first time, it becomes absolutely clear that **witnessing is the essence of meditation**. We will understand this fact better if we remind ourselves what the true goal of incarnation of the souls in the body is. Its chief task is to preserve awareness of itself, in the most restricting circumstances possible. During the course of incarnation it "matures", making itself aware of itself, and when it succeeds in becoming aware of itself in all possible states in which the body and the mind could exist, then the consciousness of the soul becomes independent from the body and the mind; that is, it recognizes its timeless independency, its true nature which connects it to the divine. This is called awakening or enlightenment. All of this shows that the soul is essentially the witness of life; it has never been fully incarnated in the body and identified with it. If consciousness is one with the body and the mind it can never be objectively aware of them. Only because it is never completely in the body and the mind, it can act as the witness of the body and the mind; we can have awareness of the body and the mind because that awareness comes from the soul. Man's awakening, culture and all of the evolution of mankind boil down to making the body aware, and all events within the body - learning to master the body and matter in general.

The same thing happens in meditation. We become aware of our body, feelings and mind, and in doing so we realize that we are neither the body, nor the mind, but the consciousness which goes beyond them. That is how we become awakened. With meditation we only get to speed up the process, because of which life itself exists together with all our incarnations. The process is accelerated only with the awareness of it, the awareness of witnessing.

Only then is **dharana** possible - focus and commitment to one goal, to meditation, to the awareness of oneself; only then do we have one I and one goal to work on (the "magnetic centre" that Gurdjieff teaches). When we experience, even for a moment, consciousness of the soul, we know what to strive for in life, from then to eternity.

When, definitely and through pratyahara, we become aware that our essence is an independent witness of all the happenings of this world, of body and mind, only then can we become aware of our true nature, and what we should strive for; this is the only goal in making the witnessing of the independent transcendental consciousness of the soul more powerful.

Only then does **dhyana** become possible – meditation, an occasional but systematic and well-practiced experience of *samadhi*, of the Self, the pure alertness or consciousness of the transcendental soul while we sit in a meditative exercise.

Having taken all the previous steps, **samadhi** becomes possible - the outcome of meditation, which is not occasional, but a permanent and timeless state of realization of the Self or consciousness of the soul, in all aspects of life.

Without the fulfillment of these prerequisites, a person cannot sit calmly for five minutes, and even less so achieve the goal of meditation. Of course, these preconditions cannot be fulfilled first, before the practice of meditation commences. They are fulfilled together with the first attempts in meditation. Meditation is a departure from the linear timeline, and for that reason all of these exist in parallel (all realities exist in parallel), all preconditions and goals of meditation we experience and realize in parallel. Actually, the goal of meditation is realized when it is properly implemented; until that moment there are only attempts in mastering meditation, together with ethical mastering, which can take years and years to achieve.

Because they are necessary for man's self-awareness, these ethical and physiological preconditions for meditation and spiritual realization in the New Age are systematically suppressed and negated through the promotion of New Age sects and various "techniques" of meditation and "spiritual technologies". That is why people today cannot sit calmly in meditation. The reason for this is a completely disturbed life in man and among people. This disruption is imposed on people systematically and in a pre-planned manner, through media, education and politics, through waging perpetual warfare and confrontation, and through poisons in food, water and medications. That is why ready-made solutions are on offer with new techniques, where everything is faster, better and easier; techniques which render any personal effort needless, and where sacrifice is not necessary in the way it was in ancient times; there is not even a mention of the ethical code.

Here we are going to correct this deficiency.

FOUR DIMENSIONS OF THE PRACTICE OF ATTENTION
VIPASSANA AND SATIPATTHÂNA

We have already seen which dimensions nature is made up of, in the description of four elements. Their different vibrations create different densities and time speeds that shape the entire cosmos. They are microcosmically compressed in a human being in the forms constituting his physical body: (earth), feelings (water), general states of mind, will or intent (fire), and his every thought (air). *From all the dimensions of the cosmos man is created, and he must therefore construct his wakefulness (through meditation) in accordance with all of them; no other method is possible.*

Therefore, one must deepen alertness in a fourfold way, regarding the:
(1) body
(2) feelings
(3) general states of mind, will or intent
(4) thoughts

These are the four foundations on which attention in meditation needs to be constantly focused, and consolidated in an attempt to understand each one separately. Each of these dimensions is dissolved from the illusion of substantiality by conscious knowledge, until they all come to their final outcome - *akasha*. When done with all of them, jointly, permanent wakefulness or pure consciousness arises.

There are various methods of meditation, but all of them are incomplete in comparison to the Buddhist method. Every other type of meditation focuses on just one of the dimensions of human existence, or simply implements mind control with the help of mantras, bodies, or emotions. They are all one-sided and incomplete, so their effects are also one-sided; they can even be harmful if they are practised for a long period of time. Their one-sidedness is often compensated by some ideology or fanaticism. Only here is the Buddhist practice comprehensively detailed, not allowing room for any ideology or religious fanaticism and unilateralism.

Man's life is unconscious and imbalanced to such a degree that he does not realize what determines him and what he is made of; he almost never distinguishes between the nature of his mental attitude from his feelings and his physical state; when he does, it is only temporary and without permanent establishment. The interdependence of these composing conditions forces the consciousness to identify with them and with the contents of their experiences of the world around us. Their **understanding through mutual distinction** will balance them entirely of their own accord, and balance the flows of life energy (prâna) in each dimension, releasing the presence of consciousness of the soul in the process. Nothing is necessary for this to take place but objective understanding. It happens in two phases.

The first phase is discernment (viveka) and the ability to tell the four dimensions of our existence apart, and by getting to know each of them individually; the dimensions prior to this point had been able to work interdependently, and therefore with a conditioning effect on one another. For such differentiation we need permanent or **constant attention**, an objective awareness of our own being and everything that is happening within it. This is the meaning of the word *satipatthâna*.

The second phase is the ability to **apply insight (*vipassana*)** of these four composing parts spontaneously, in the same way they happen in life. Constant attention all by itself means very little without making sense of what is observed. Applying insights leads to the practical strengthening of consciousness of the soul, in all of the activities of our body and mind. Vipassana is here, according to the original Buddha's teachings, applied in all the dimensions human beings are made of: (1) body - earth, (2) feelings - water, (3) general states of mind, will or intention - fire, and (4) every thought - air.[8]

It must be emphasized here that Buddha stresses that in every segment of exercise, the focus of attention should be on the given object only. If that object is the body, then all focus should be on the body; if it is breathing, then breathing only, feelings only, and so on. It must not be mixed with other objects of practice while it deals with one object; it must stick to its object only. This is important because of their distinction. The awareness is the distinction. Buddha says that our task is to become aware of 'the body in the body', 'feelings in feelings', 'states of mind in states of mind' - here and now, without any abstract interference.

The distinction between all of the factors that constitute us is crucial for awakening or realizing con-

---

[8] For more detailed instructions on practising the insight of vipassana, see the works of Satya Narayan Goenka. A very useful book by William Hart: "The Art of Living: Vipassana Meditation, As Taught by S. N. Goenka." The problem is, however, that the practice of vipassana meditation in Goenka teaching is limited to the body and breathing only, although it does still have some beneficial effects. More details on how to become aware of emotions can be found in the John Ruskan book: "Emotional Clearing: Releasing Negative Feelings and Awakening Unconditional Happiness."

sciousness of the soul. We are never conscious enough of the effect the body has on the mind, mind on the body, feelings on the mind and the body - the way they are all intricately woven with one another. It is, actually, this bond that ties our soul to our body, which conditions our consciousness; the inability to distinguish, which in turn creates the inability to understand what constitutes us.

Ignorance about what truly makes us creates all the remaining misunderstandings, both in people and in interpersonal relationships. When we learn to distinguish between what makes us, then we learn to tell the difference, and we become aware of all other misunderstandings. Contemporary psychology and psychotherapy deal with this. Only when we establish and learn to distinguish between all these connections and their mutual conditions can we be objectively conscious of our existence, can we be free, and that means having full consciousness of the soul.

1. Awareness of the body

The body is a collective place for all the phenomena of the being, for all feelings and mental states. Therefore, in order to be aware of feelings and the mind, we firstly have to be perfectly aware of the body. When we are overwhelmed with feelings and mental activity, we forget about the body, so it remains the most unconscious area of existence, even though it provides the base for it. We are always more aware of what we imagine than our breathing or of tiny movements of the face and hands. In order for this fundamental oblivion of being to be overcome and consciousness, for the first time in life, to unite with its being, with all bodily actions, we need to link it to breath.

a) Focus attention on breath

The awareness of breathing acts like a plumb bob that directs attention to the body and dissuades it from the swaying of psycho-mental contents and outer objects. Focusing attention on the breath keeps consciousness centred on the objective perception of the totality of any phenomenon, on the body, and discourages it from the old habit of being seduced by the abstract contents of peculiar events. Here is the beginning of complete dissuasion of the soul from the conditioned way of living in time; being fully aware of breathing keeps us in the present moment, in reality, here and now. That is why it needs to be well implemented. The focus of attention on breathing, independent from other exercises, brings abundant fruits in spiritual purification, if applied persistently. This practice is sufficient in itself, because it directly causes distraction of the soul from the interference of natural events and with due perseverance it can lead to the soul recognizing its complete independence from the body. Namely, breathing is an automatic, natural process. With its awareness, we realize that it is not our process; we cannot stop it, we realize that we are not breathing, but that nature breathes in the shape of "our" body, and that there is nothing that is ours. That is how we enhance the consciousness of independence of the soul from the body. Therefore, *the essence of becoming aware of breathing is in the realization that we are not breathing ourselves; breathing is one of the spontaneous processes of wholeness; nature itself breathes through "our" body. We are only a witness to this.* The insight that shows that no breath is ours is the beginning of all wisdom.

(Aside from attaching attention to breathing, there are other methods to distract the consciousness from the contents of our thoughts and the objective world. This can be done by concentrating on a certain shape, such as *yantra*, or on a certain word, *mantra*. Although they are efficient, these methods are connected to tradition and ideology, while the awareness of breathing is independent from all ideologies and beliefs, and is naturally available to every man.)

The practice should be completed in a secluded and peaceful place, a couple of times a day, for at least half an hour, sitting in the upright position but comfortably. We should perceive breathing with an alert mind and without any disturbance, just the way it happens naturally. We should establish awareness of each inhalation and exhalation quite clearly, when the breath is shorter, and when it is longer. Breath should be followed either by its flow upward into the nostrils or by movement of the breasts and stomach. It would be best to do both. The establishment is done indifferently, without any mental interference or judgment. The awareness of breathing serves to distract the consciousness from the constant and burdensome attachment to its psychic contents, that are related to personal experience or the world, past or future; and the calming should be experienced as the innocence of the being itself, which is relaxed and composed, and breathes here and now. Breathing is the way we return to the true innocence of our being, a blessed existence, a timeless present, and liberate ourselves from all the burdens of life's experience. With each inhalation the body needs to become more conscious, with each exhalation more relaxed and calmer. This is the basic requirement of this practice.

In the basic text of Buddha's teaching on contemplation and meditation in general, *Sati-patthana-sutta* (D. 22 i M. 10), the initial question is: "How does a monk conduct the practice of observing the body in the body?" Hav-

155

ing gone into the woods, at the foot of some tree, or in an empty room, the monk sits with his legs crossed and with his body in the upright position, with constant attention. He inhales with full attention, he exhales with full attention. By inhaling the long breath he knows: 'I am inhaling the long breath'; by inhaling the short breath he knows: 'I am inhaling the short breath'. By exhaling the long breath he knows: 'I am exhaling the long breath'; by exhaling the short breath he knows: 'I am exhaling the short breath'. 'I will inhale by being conscious of the entire body' is how the practice is done; 'I will exhale by being conscious of the entire body' is how the practice is done; 'I will inhale while calming down bodily functions' is how the practice is done; 'I will exhale while calming down bodily functions' is how the practice is done.

b) Basic positions of the body

The awareness of the surface of the whole body that's acquired during the half-hour practice of attention on breathing must be kept in everyday motion. In order to achieve this, we firstly need to develop the ability to always remain conscious of four basic positions: walking, standing, sitting, and lying. Each of these basic positions must be clearly established, and the transition from one to the other must be carried out as a preconceived conscious intention.

c) All movements

When we, without effort, become aware of the changing between the four basic positions throughout the day, we can move on to empowering the presence of attention on the more important movements we make with our bodies. (The smallest, in the beginning, are not important for the practice). When we change direction when walking; when we look straight ahead, and when we look aside; when we bend and when we stretch out our limbs; when we get dressed and undressed; what we carry in our hands; while we eat, drink, chew and experience taste, and swallow; when we perform physiological needs of the body; when we are about to fall asleep and when we wake up; when we talk and when we are silent, we invariably apply focus.

In order to practice awareness of all movement without too much effort, it is a good idea in the beginning to practice **meditation in walking**. This is done in a special room where there are no disturbances, travelling along a certain path. Fully conscious, we slowly tread, step by step, conscious of all the phases of walking, the feeling of pressure from heel to toes, aware of the space around us, the sounds, light and other occurrences if any. Together with all this, we remain constantly aware of our breath.

By establishing all the described procedures we gain a clear insight into the purposefulness and justification of each process, whether it is a product of mechanism or habit, or objectively justified; and in doing so we stop losing energy on unnecessary and often meaningless activities. Then we gain a clear insight into the most appropriate way of performing each process, in accordance with current circumstances, independently from acquired habits and customs, impetuosity and desires. The awareness itself directs the correctness in all procedures. The establishment of all procedures of the body keeps us composed or self-conscious in everything we do throughout the day; each activity can be and must be included in the focus of attention, at least in its basic elements. There is no activity of the body that cannot be the subject of conscious attention. If we are victims of some compulsory and unfavourable activity or habits, conscious attention will definitely remove them. It is impossible to do anything disadvantageous or badly while being fully aware of consciousness of the soul. Consciousness itself removes all bad activities.

For the first time in our life, we reach cognition with these practices: "I am the doer of every movement and action." This is the integration of consciousness, which is above the body and senses, merging into one I. This means that the mind is simultaneously integrated. Up until that moment, awareness of oneself was there, but the mind was so disintegrated and engaged with its assorted contents - split into multiple I's - it rendered such consciousness weak and passive; it was not present in its entirety, as the decisive and key factor. ***With constant awareness of our movements, we strengthen the one I in ourselves, making our mind complete. Then we also become responsible for everything we do.*** Prior to that moment, we were not accountable for anything; everything was done by our unconscious nature with the help of a divided and passive mind. But when we come to one I, then we become responsible for our actions, because for the first time we have the power to act. We are only a creator of thoughts, words and deeds with responsible awareness of our own being; we acquire objective consciousness of ourselves, which makes us realize that the one who is the doer is as conditioned as his deeds. This is the way to recognize the truth that each individual creation in nature is dependent, unstable and transient, while consciousness of the soul, which observes, is independent from the body and its actions. Therefore, complete awareness and establishing the psychophysical factor (body and mind) eventually lead us to overcome it, because consciousness is always the act of overcoming the established contents the unconsciousness has been identifying with. In such a manner, the full integration of awareness of action leads to overcoming subjective identification with the doer (body and mind). It is important to understand that this overcoming happens as a consequence of previously acquired maturity, and responsibility on the part of the subject for his own actions, and that maturity is best expressed as the overcoming of subjectivity. The subject who identifies with himself can never have responsibility for his actions, nor objective awareness of them. Only when the body and the mind become fully conscious can the consciousness of the soul in us become objectively aware of the body, and able to recognize its independence from it.

If consciousness of our soul were in unison with the body, it could not be different from its actions. The possibility of becoming aware of the body proves to the consciousness of the soul that it is independent from the body; and in this way, it awakens the soul to its authentic state.

Identification of consciousness with the body induces the effort of concentration, which is not meditation. In this case, the consciousness tirelessly divides itself into the observer and the observed, and a committed act. The lack of responsibility and objectivity will act as a witness to such a schizoid split. The effect of consciousness can be seen in our ability to change all of our habits in movement and thinking, in finding enough strength to abandon them, as well as experiencing adequate participation in them.

By abandoning identification of man's soul with the body, feelings and mind, activities take place purposefully, with even more powerful and purer energy and intelligence. For an independent soul, the movement of the body and thoughts belong to the same domain as all other natural phenomena. Nature has never displayed itself as being so healthy and complete in its perfection as in the unconstrained view of a separate and independent soul of man. The question of whether nature achieves its purpose and perfection with an awakening of the unconditioned soul in man, or whether man awakens only when he begins to perceive the true perfection and completeness of nature, is redundant. Because of the relativity of the time of natural occurrences, both of these events are mutual, they happen at the same time because they are equally real. There is no essential difference in whether nature becomes perfect only in an awakened man, or he becomes awakened because he has realized the perfection of nature. In the moment of awakening, the whole period of development of nature gets compressed into one single event.

d) Detachment from the body

The more we sense freedom, the more the soul is detached from the body, its own being. Strengthened objective consciousness is of such quality that it starts to identify the soul with the body less and less, it idealizes the body less and less; it perceives it the way it truly is, no longer whole and reliable, but a biological mechanism locked within the boundaries of skin, consisting of different organs: bones, flesh, intestines, liver, heart, lungs, kidneys, blood, urine, sputum, feces, hair, nails, teeth, brain, and more. Like a bag filled with various objects.

In this way we should, at least once a day, look at our body, and use our spirit to dissect it into its organic parts without emotion. We should not only treat it as a living organism, but as a corpse that goes through all the phases of decay - something that will inevitably happen to it. We should envisage this moment quite clearly. In such a manner, the soul will slowly detach from its ties to the body, together with any unnecessary repulsion toward the body. One who always has death on his mind, in this objective way, will not make a mistake, he will not lose time, he will always perceive life as it is, because he will always experience it fully and with love.

e) Awareness of the basic elements of the body

At the end of focusing our attention on the body, there is an insight about the basic elements that compose the thing we consider our body to be. This is a more subtle form of detachment than the previous one. Those are the elements of earth, water, fire and air. They symbolically depict the basic properties of matter: strength, grip, warmth and movement. An objective and impersonal look at the body reveals that a being is their combination only in action; it can always be recognized as such. We need to recognize our body in this way more often, until it becomes one and only. In this way, we will see the unity of the body with nature in all of its dimensions, which are represented with the same elements.

The practice of making the body aware should be done as described above. In doing so, we need to have the origin of our body always on our mind; the spontaneous actions of causative formation of everything in nature and food, the circulation of prâna. While doing so, we should not confuse the object of our focus with other areas of the being, with feelings or states of mind for which there are special exercises; they refer to the body, exclusively. Only with its awareness does the consciousness need to be expanded, with the following exercise. In order to make the higher dimensions of the being more aware (chiefly feelings and thoughts) we firstly need to consciously master the basis of their occurrence, with the body itself. At the beginning it is good to practise the focus of attention intensively in all aspects (a, b, c, d, e – each individually) only at a certain time during the day, in chosen conditions, whereby movements can be performed slowly so attention is more easily kept on them. When awareness of all bodily phenomena becomes present easily, it can be incorporated into the process, so that others are unable to notice it. While doing so, we should not force attention, nor adjust our movements, merely maintain their unison. What happens should be the subject of alert observation: when walking, we should be just walking, when doing something with our hands, then we should be doing something with our hands, when speaking speech, and when sitting and doing nothing, then sitting and breathing.

Full awareness of the body will be made easy if we constantly attach our attention to the centre of its events; the gravitational centre in the lower abdomen (when we find ourselves in the basic positions of the body), as well as the whole surface of the body (with all other movements). The characteristic of unconscious functioning of the body is its instability with regards to its natural centre. The focus of its action is raised upwards, towards the head and thoughts, and therefore it is off-balance, like a distorted wheel where the axis is not properly fixed at the centre. In the gravitational centre of the being, the vital energy finds its support for movement and flow through the entire body. When that process of action from the centre is crystallized by consciousness, time of its implementation is faster, manifested in the form of more energy and the power for realization.

The previous description of practising presence of consciousness (under a, b, c, d, e) and centring in the gravitational centre, represents only the inner and therefore a very incomplete method of making the being conscious. Consciousness of the soul in our being becomes complete only when it gets its external expression, which is shown by moving through space (walking, driving, etc.); we always have a deep experience that we, with our focus, consciousness of the soul, are not moving, but remain absolutely immovable, while all of space, all the beings and the entire universe are moving and spinning round in our proximity.

Consciousness of the soul in us is always recognized as a timeless presence, independent from space.

The meditation of movement is complete only with the realization that no being is moving with his/her own will, but instead are integrating part of the general movement of the cosmos, which is nature in motion, and every movement we make flows along the general movement of life energy (*prana*), in the way a leaf flows down a stream.

This belief of non-action in the middle of the action process should be realized while practising awareness of feelings and the mind, as though they move following a set path of their own destiny, and not by our will. Complete authenticity and independence of consciousness of the soul will be manifested when we clearly experience that our essence or soul does not move in the events throughout life, that it even never participated in them; but the body, feelings, moods or states of mind, and all thoughts happen on their own, and they move along their own path in the shapes of nature, orchestrated by the same laws as everything else in nature. With the achievement of the final differentiation of consciousness of the soul and nature, this state will be permanent and natural.

The focus of attention on the body is applied by man himself first, and then on the others intermittently, and then simultaneously both on himself and on others. The more aware we are of our actions, the better we will be able to detect the degree of other people's unawareness, and we will notice the difference in nobility which consciousness brings, from the misery and ugliness unconsciousness generates. The main characteristic of a conscious body is relaxation and uniformity of speech and all movements. The consciousness harmonizes all the energy flows, by annulling all passions, and such a man starts to have a soothing effect on the people around him.

The focus of attention on the body is successful to the level it manages to strengthen the independence of the soul from the body. Its purpose is to achieve the **ability to preserve the presence of transcendental, independent soul, in all possible events and tendencies of the body, in all the states the body can be found**. The essence of this exercise is that consciousness can free itself from all imaginary images of the body, and bring the insight that there is no other physical survival than the one described here. That is why the focus of attention on the body needs to be established, until all illusions of other types of survival disappear, and the only thing that remains is what's described here, always perfectly clear in man's direct insight.

Having realized that it is all the activity of nature and not his own, man is no longer worried about things that are not his; he is not attached to the physical form which lives in the world; for the same reason he ceases to experience repulsion towards the world and towards the body, he is indifferent and calm in the independence of his own purification (*kaivalya*).

2. Awareness of feelings

A somewhat finer dimension of the body are feelings, which are different from the rough physical body. They are directly tied to the experience of bodily phenomena. There are only three states in which feelings are expressed: pleasant, painful and neutral. Each of these states can be mundane, connected with life in the world as such (sensual nature), or exalted, which means inclined to detachment from the conditioned being which lives in this world (spiritual nature). Similar to the physical body, the astral body (whose actions we are talking about here) can show an inkling of something during its movement (because of the pleasant state), repulsive (due to some painful experience) or neutral (in some periods).

Here, it is not about emotions, or getting to know their endless irresolvable complexities, but about the feelings themselves, here and now. Problematic emotions are always complex creations which occur only when mixing feelings with physical events, general states of mind, will and certain mental contents, which are the subject of special practice here.

One should always clearly recognize which feeling is in question: if it is pleasant, painful or neutral; if it is a pleasant common feeling, or a pleasant sublime feeling (e.g. satisfaction because of an insight into the reality of being and independence of the soul); if it is a painful common or a painful sublime feeling (regretting one's weaknesses that hinder salvation); whether it is a neutral common or a neutral sublime feeling (indifference owing to insight into the independence of soul and the permanent quality of the outcome of all existence).

This is how the focus or permanent presence of attention on oneself and on others is practised - usually by noticing the differences in nobility and tranquility when feelings are clearly established in us, according to the described model, and the example of misery they cause in other people when they are mixed up and identified with contents of the mind and physical experiences. One has to bear in mind these factors in the origin of feelings, and this represents the causal occurrence of everything in nature, desires and sensual impressions, as well as the disintegration of all of these factors over time. Feelings are, like the body, unstable and transient, which is why we need to get rid of the illusion of their permanence. We practise by envisaging to ourselves the following: "In me, there is such a feeling now". During the pleasant feeling we need to abandon the tendency to be greedy; in an unpleasant feeling we need to abandon the tendency toward repulsion and hate; and in neutral feelings we need to abandon the tendency for dumb laziness. In this way feelings are established - they occur all by themselves in everyday experience, and we should not wander onto other subjects or lose the focus of our attention (on the body, state of mind); we should rather stick to the feelings chosen as the subject. That is why there are no other feelings than those described here; we should distinguish between them clearly, and establish them for as long as it takes for illusions regarding various feelings and their properties to disappear, illusions which occur with the confusing mixing of feelings of the mind and bodily states, until only the ones described here remain, always clear upon insight.

Clear insight, proving that there are no other feelings except for those described here, boils down to the realization of what feelings actually are. They are the same as thoughts, although a little slower and with denser vibrations. Thoughts are the finest vibrations of the phenomena of nature, turned into the informative conception of events. This designing happens in our body, because it was originally made to be a suitable place for this. But the body itself is too fast and unstable; it is current, it needs some connecting tissue, a material which will act as cement or glue in preserving consciousness for the long-term creation of information, for the possibility of comparison with other information in time and space. Feelings do just this. Therefore, they are also informative vibrations, albeit slower and changed with more difficulty. They are good as a binding material; feelings not only help us to see content deeper, but also enable the option to see it from more aspects, related to other contents; the problem is that emotions bind all impressions, so that each man has more or less emotional trauma from the past, which he picked up while growing up. Because of the nature of feelings, we tend to relyon them more than necessary, and experience them from several aspects, which is sometimes necessary but quite often completely redundant. That is the true nature of traumas. With objective establishment of feelings and emotions in the way they truly are, at the present moment, all emotional traumas from the past that keep blocking us are resolved.

The focus of attention on feelings, the way they are, without judgement, will be successful to the degree it is able to empower the independence of the soul from feelings; its ability to stay detached from anything living in space and time, as well as **not getting attached to repulsion in regards to anything;** its indifference and calmness during the process of purification. Its purpose is to achieve the **ability to preserve transcendental, independent consciousness of the soul, in all possible phenomena and feelings, in all the states where emotions can be found.**

3. Awareness of general states of mind or expressions of will

As the first two practices to establish attention deal exclusively with movement and survival of the body, on both the rougher (physical) and finer levels (feelings), in the same way the following two practices deal with the rougher (general) and finer (individual) states of mind, which are manifested as intentions or expressions of will.

The manifestation of will or intention starts from the smallest decision, when we want to do something, like move our body at any given moment, right up until the moment we decide to do something momentous that has far-reaching consequences; a job that is a product of our current state of mind or mood.

When **lust** appears in our mind, we need to establish it clearly, and when there is no lust, we should establish its absence; when **hate** appears, we need to establish it clearly, and when there is none, we need to indicate its absence; when **misconceptions**[9] appear in our mind, we need to clearly establish such states, and when there are none, we should enhance the clarity with which the consciousness illuminates the subject or the object of its perception (body, feelings or mind) without deceptions which unite it with the basic qualities that do not exist, and divert it from the reality of the object or phenomenon.

Lust (attachment), hatred (repulsion) and misconception (ignorance or unconsciousness) are the three basic states of mind and directions of will that enslave man.

Likewise, when anxiety appears in the mind, we should clearly establish that it is anxiety (from something

---

[9] Misconceptions are memories, fantasies, and the act of imposing imaginary characteristics on subjects and events.

particular that causes worry and inhibition of the mind); when distractions happen, that they are a distraction (due to the unfavourable influence of a multitude of contents or objects, which cause anxiety and a constant need for change); when expanded consciousness appears in the mind, we should be aware that it is the consciousness which originates from the experience of a three-dimensional body (written or extrasensory information, memory, idea, acquired knowledge from far away places, past or future); when narrowed consciousness appears, we should know that consciousness has been narrowed (to some specific outlook, from the immediate surroundings and in the present moment); when our mind experiences consciousness that goes beyond sensory perception and starts to move to astral, that is the consciousness which overcomes bodily experience (during visions or astral projection); and when consciousness which does not go beyond the physical experience is on our mind, this is the type of consciousness which is dependent on the body and senses; when the mind focuses on what goes on, we should become aware of the fact that it is focused, and when it is out of focus, consciousness splits itself into multiple processes that keep changing; when consciousness is freed from all the contents with which the mind is conditioned (in meditation, *dhyânam*), we should be aware that it is free (from thoughts, and is present in the being without them), and when it is not free, we should clearly establish that it is not free, but is conditioned with thoughts (which objects can cause in the mind - beyond contemplative absorption, *dhyânam*).

That is how the focus of attention is improved in all general states in which the mind can find itself. In this way, we should establish them for as long as the illusion that states of mind can be different exist - until these illusions finally begin to disappear, and the only thing that remains is what has been stated here, always on display for knowledge and clear insight.[10] Only in this way can we achieve the purpose of this exercise, which enables man to recognize independence from all states of mind and expressions of will. Awareness is applied on oneself and others, intermittently, and then simultaneously on oneself and others. In doing so, there can clearly be seen the difference between the conscious states in us, and their unconscious rotation in others. We need to notice the change in state of mind in ourselves, when the mind is found in a sublime and conscious state, and when it is in a low and unconscious state. Then, we need to remember and connect those moments of exaltation and heightened awareness, and on the basis of that connection, the periods of decreasing consciousness will be recognized more clearly and thus they will be shortened in duration, until they disappear. We should also clearly see the factors which enable the mind, which represent the overall activity of a naturally formed body, the ignorance of independence and the desire for personal participation in life within a certain timeframe, and that the mind will survive for as long as its factors are joined together.

Awareness of all the general states of mind is successful to the degree that it enables recognition of *the independence of man's soul from all the possible states in which the mind can find itself, by implementing its will through the mind, its non-attachment to the world of objects, as well as non-attachment to repulsion of the world of objects and the mind;* to the degree it is able to strengthen its indifferent presence in freedom, which enables both the world of objects and the mind.

---

[10] There are, apart from these three basic, ten in total.

4. Awareness of the causes of the creation of each individual's mental contents (of every thought)

In this fourth dimension of vipassana, the presence of wakefulness is finally purified from the finest interference between mental contents and personal experiences.

Unlike the neutral establishment of awareness, the suspension of established causes that are unfavourable is required here, and the encouragement of favourable ones is needed. Therefore, the permanent takeover of responsibility and free will are now the requirement.

The causes of all kinds of thoughts are divided into favourable and unfavourable ones, as there are favourable and unfavourable psychophysical experiences (*karma*).

The unfavourable causes are represented here as five obstacles, five types of adhesion, and six internal and six external basic senses; while the favourable causes are the seven factors of awakening and four of basic truths of the nature of existence that unite and reveal the outcome of events in general.

a) Five main obstacles (*nivarana*) that interfere with the liberation of consciousness from mental contents

The first obstacle is the ***desire for sensory experience*** through any of the six senses (reason or the mind is regarded here as the sixth sense). When any sensory desire arises, we should clearly identify it as such, and when there is none, we should establish that there is none. We should ascertain how the still non-existent desire for sensory experience arises and affects thoughts, how the already existing sensual desire evaporates and does not reappear in the future - taking the thoughts based on them with them.

The second obstacle is ***anger and grouchiness***. When it occurs, we should clearly identify it as such, and when there is none, we should become aware of its absence. We should observe the way in which impending anger and grouchiness occur and take over thoughts, how the existing anger dissolves and does not reappear in the future, as do those thoughts which are less than merciful.

The third obstacle is ***laziness and sluggishness***. We should establish them clearly when they are present and when they are not, how they occur and shape thinking, as well as how to abandon them so they do not reappear in the future.

The fourth obstacle is a***nxiety and concern for survival***. When these appear we should establish them clearly as such and regard how they influence our thinking, and when they are not present we should clearly establish that the mind is free of them. We should clearly notice how impending concern appears and influences the mind, how existing concerns go away and do not reappear in the future.

The fifth and the most difficult cause of psycho-mental conditioning occurs as a ***suspicion that freedom is possible*** or that it exists at all. Whenever such a suspicion occurs, we need to identify it clearly, and when there is none, see that it has gone and remain firm. We should see how impending suspicion arises, how the existing suspicion leaves us, and how abandoned suspicion no longer appears.

This is how you practice the focus of attention on the five obstacles which are the cause of all psycho-mental conditioning, in oneself and in others, intermittently and simultaneously. In doing so, we have to bear in mind that the causes of these obstacles are natural conditioning and fickleness. The practice must be done in the manner described, to the point it starts to enable a comprehensive insight into these obstacles, and the realization that there are no other obstacles to the purification of consciousness of the soul from psycho-mental conditioning but these five. This is the way man liberates consciousness of the soul from attachments to the manifested world, as well as repulsion regarding the world, calming it down in the process of spiritual purification.

b) Five types of adherence to the existence of the body

There are five types of mutual adherence, which together make the creation (*skandha*) which temporarily assumes the personality of an average individual's body, or the empirical experience of I, the belief, "I am the body". Connected to them, individual consciousness (*jiva*) causes rebirth and maintains individual life experiences.

The first adherence refers to the **material form of the body** (*rűpa-skandhâ*). We need to clearly envisage how the body is created by acquiring the necessary conditions for creation, how it survives in ever-changing conditions, and how it disappears, so that attachment to it can be abandoned.

The second adherence refers to **sensory abilities** (*vedana skandhâ*). These are: hearing, sight, touch, taste, smell and thinking (reason). It must be made clear how sensory abilities are created and how they survive conditioning, and how they disappear, in order for attachment to them to be abandoned as well.

The third adherence refers to **observation** (*samdjna*) based on the six senses (*buddhindriye* and *manas*). We need to clearly envisage the nature of our observations, how they occur depending on the senses, and how they disappear along with them. This is how adherence to un-

173

stable and conditioned sensory observations will be abandoned, and consciousness will become independent from their limited functionality.

The fourth adherence occurs in the form of **expressing incentive or will for reactive action** (*karmendriye*) based on a subconscious dependence on individual sensory perception (buddhindriye). We should clearly establish how each unconscious reaction (samskara) is an expression for activity of the body (to do something at a given moment), conditioned by the scope of sensory experience; how it comes about and how it disappears. Then we should notice that the will for conditioned reaction and action is maintained with the illusion that we will be at a loss if we do not satisfy it; this does not refer to obsessions and habits (physical action), but, in a milder form, thoughts. With such insight, all incentives for participation in transient and unstable existence are abandoned.

The fifth adherence refers to **identification of the consciousness with the mind** (*manas*), its conclusions, concepts and conceptions. Such consciousness (vijnana) is directly dependent on the area of sensory experience. This dependency of consciousness on the mind needs to be clearly established when it exists, how it occurs should be witnessed, as should how it disappears. Only in this way can man set himself free from the attachment to an unstable and dependent empirical mind.

This is how we practice the focus of attention on the five types of adherence which condition and hinder clear consciousness of the soul in the body, and which always act together in a group as a temporary entity in the form of the 'I' (ego). There are no other factors of empirical 'I' except for these five adherents, and only when they are together does 'I' survive in its recognizable form. As long as this group is unaware, that is before this practice where I is disintegrated and divided, it can never be whole, because its life energy is out of balance and invested in various attachments, depending on the circumstances and induced behavior of the body. With this kind of awareness, for the first time 'I' becomes integrated through balancing out energy flows, and becomes a complete personality (*aham-kâra*) which goes beyond any inauthentic attachment to the body (indriyâni). Integration and individuality of the personality (aham-kâra) have no other purpose but to overcome individual separation (indriyâni) liberating man from all obstacles which tie the soul in him.[11]

We should clearly establish in ourselves and then in others, intermittently as well as simultaneously, how all of these attachments interact, where the movement of one (body) pulls the others (feelings and mind) to become manifested as 'I'. We need to practice, consistently and in the way described, until we achieve insight into how fivefold adherence works as a cause of mental conditionality, and discover that there is no adherence of man other than an inauthentic existence in the form of adherence to the body.

c) Six inner and six outer bases of the senses

The next cause of mental contents is related to the connection between sensory abilities (*buddhindriye*) and their outer prototypes (*tanmâtrâ*).

Here they are established as reciprocal: the eye with visible shapes, ear with sound, nose with smells, tongue with tastes, body with touch, and mind with the

---

[11] See my book "Sankhya - The Ancient Science of Nature and the Human Soul". The complete context of meditation is presented on the pages of this book.

objects of the mind (physical or imaginary). We should clearly see how each of these sensory abilities exist inseparably from its outer bases, and how together they create the **ten chains** for consciousness that enslave the free soul of man:

    1. Belief in the steadfastness of the body and the mind in it
    2. Suspiciousness of liberation
    3. Belief in the possibility of liberation based on metaphysics, dogmas, morals and rituals
    4. Passion
    5. Malice and hatred
    6. Longing for existence in ideal conditions, in this world and in this body
    7. Longing for eternal existence in ideal celestial worlds (astral)
    8. Vanity
    9. Anxiety
    10. Ignorance of the unconditioned soul as the immanent outcome of all existence

    These ten chains of consciousness can appear through uncontrolled perception via any of the six senses. We should clearly establish how the non-existent chain appears, and how the already existing chain is abandoned, so that the abandoned chain does not reappear in the future.
    This contemplation is done within oneself and in others, intermittently and simultaneously. The causes of the physical bases of the senses are: ignorance, the desire for existence in time, food, and the general characteristics of the causative formation of everything in nature. The senses will go on existing until the decomposition of

these factors. Such awareness sets man free from desires regarding the world, and from grief because of experiences in the world, enabling him to recognize the presence of an independent soul in him, and in everything.

d) Seven factors of the soul's awakening in the body

There are seven factors that are purifying to consciousness of the soul and that awaken man from all the contents of psycho-mental conditioning:

1) **Focus of attention** (*satipatthâna*, the meditation practice described here, the awareness of the four dimensions of being). We should always know when it is present and when it is not, we should clearly establish how the still non-existent focus of attention occurs, and how occurred attention is empowered further to perfection, so that it is always present.

2) Through the focus of attention reality is explored and insight into the nature of all physical and mental phenomena is empowered. We should clearly see the difference when the **exploration of reality**, as the factor of awakening, is present and when it is not, and clearly establish how the research begins and develops.

3) As a consequence of a deeper insight into reality, the **will** for independence, the third factor of awakening, grows stronger. This will should be noticed consciously, when it is present and when it is not, how non-existent will develops with the strengthening of insight, and how already existing will is empowered further to perfection.

4) Strengthened will for independence causes growing spiritual **rapture** and pleasantness, due to a clear vision of the transcendental soul, the only possible outcome and freedom. And rapture, as a factor of awakening, needs to be established - when it is present and when it is

not, how rapture starts with the focus of attention, and how existing rapture is empowered until we achieve blissful freedom.

5) Once man recognizes the freedom and independence of consciousness of the soul, the body calms and the mind becomes quiet. Then **calmness of the body and the mind**, as the fifth factor of awakening of the soul, is strengthened. We should clearly establish how this quieting is achieved, when it is present and when it is not, and how, based on the previous factors, it is strengthened.

6) When the body and the mind are quiet and silent, time and space of all the happenings are merged into one (*samadhi*), as the pure consciousness of oneself. This is the conscious *focus* (*samadhi*) of all experiences in the unity of space-time, in 'I am' as the sixth factor of awakening. It can only be realized through the practice of meditation. The unity of nature and consciousness already exists at its base, because of that unity; there is nothing new. When we bring our individual being to conscious unity, then we automatically see all of nature as one, and we do not distinguish it from ourselves, from the experience of 'I am'. It is crucial that this kind of focus (*samadhi*) is established in oneself, to clearly see the consequences of the absence of focus, to achieve non-existent focus based on previous factors, and to bring this focus to perfection.

7) When the unity of all dimensions and space-time has become a conscious event, known as the only reality of world and man in 'I am', when man clearly recognizes that consciousness as his own essence and his only destiny, as himself, then he wakefully and indifferently (*upekkha*) observes the illusion of the divided existence of a multitude of forms in time. Such **indifferent purifica-**

tion (*kaivalya*), from all the conditionalities of transient existence (*prakrti*), is the seventh factor in the realization of awakening the soul, and becomes recognized by man once and for all.

All aspects of existence (prakrti) then become equal to us, it does not happen any more that something gets to seduce our consciousness within identification less (during meditation), and some more (during action). Everything is equal, because we see that everything is just prakrti, and that we are always independent from all events (as soul or purusha). Hence the indifference.

Unlike other factors of awakening, the indifferent purification from any conditionality of existence cannot be noticed - when it is present, and when it is not - but is instead realized with the previous factors, and once achieved remains forever in man as the primary condition and consciousness of the soul within him, and existence itself in the outer world.

In this way the seven basic factors become steadily established, awakening and liberating from any psycho-mental conditioning of nature.

e) Four basic truths about existence

Only after becoming aware of the causes of all thoughts can one come to the ***first truth*** about existence: all its factors are deprived of permanent or true characteristics; instead they are composed, conditioned and inconstant, and therefore the psycho-mental connection of man to any form of existence is futile, illusory, unnatural, and therefore, in the final outcome, causes only suffering and loss, both for man and for nature.[12] Because, as already stated, the essence of nature also has and finds its meaning through an independent and transcendental soul that enables everything, through the soul of man, and it is not necessary for the soul of man to seek sanctuary in nature. The soul is the savior, it is here to enlighten and elevate nature through itself, towards the divine consciousness, and not fall and enslave itself in what it needs to elevate. If it does so, man experiences the suffering of birth and aging, sickness and dying, he is united with those he does not like, and he is dissociated from those he loves, he does not achieve what he wants, and things he does not want happen to him. In short, five types of adherences (b) of life experience cause suffering: being attached to the body, feelings, perceptions, expressions of will, and the mind. They are temporary entities of natural occurrences and they do not touch the soul of man. In themselves, these entities are not the problem, but the connection of man to them is problematic. They are only means of living, not goals. Only the inappropriate and inauthentic is painful for man; he adheres to inappropriate and transient shapes of existence, those that are the closest to him in experience, constituting the body. When he sees the wholeness of the process of nature, man does not

---

[12] Suffering as the first truth, is here shown with Buddha's term *dukha* which in the widest sense marks inauthenticity, imperfection, that without full consciousness of the soul things are never in the ideal state, but always a little different, a little imperfect, that they are never fulfilled by man's wishes. That is why Buddha uses this term, to denote the basic fact of life, that it is like the wheel (*kha*) which is inadequately (*du*) centred on the axis. Only with the spiritual effort of awareness of the soul of which we have spoken here, does life become correctly (*su*) centred and therefore pleasant (*sukha*).

adhere to them any more, because he can simultaneously see that he is independent, that it is not him and there nothing that is his, that l he can also be conscious of natural happenings as a unique whole, because his soul overcomes everything. *If the soul of man were not above the entire nature, man could never be objectively conscious of the world as a whole.*

Suffering, as the expression of ignorance of a unique natural causation and identification with it, can be triple: subjectively induced, objectively imposed, or the manifestation of destiny. If some being is happy, that happiness will only be temporary and completely dependent on its causes. We can always find more people who are not satisfied with life, who endure life more than they enjoy it - and that is why they turn to illusions. Man can only enjoy the aesthetic experience of objective nature, savour its beauties. The more relaxed and simple he is, the clearer he sees the simple beauty of nature. With complete relaxation, he can also see the ultimate truth of suffering, and that is: suffering does not have an objective reality; it is only a reaction to the forced suppression of ego and illusion by the divine. Namely, the divine cannot wait for the ego to transform and disappear by itself - because it will never go against its own self-preservation - but the divine has to create situations in which the man will be, whether he likes it or not, faced with reality; where he will overcome ego with a unity of existence in which individuals do not exist as separate. Such situations break the illusion of ego, conceptions about individuality and substantiality, and this is experienced as suffering. It, therefore, exists only for the ego. Existence itself is divine and therefore there cannot be wrong or negative. All suffering is an illusion of ego, a consequence of the wrong approach to reality, and not reality itself. If suffering were real, then there would be no place for the divine. However, due to the nature of the three-dimensional physical world, illusions of many individuals acquire accumulative power, so they may look perfectly real. Therefore, although it occurs as a product of an illusion, suffering exists and affects people.

Essentially, identification of subject with the object, with life, is suffering, because man loses a clear and stable bond with his essence, with his soul. If things were set in such a way that man can find eternal refuge, fulfillment and love in somebody else, in the outer world or in external objects, then he would completely neglect and forget himself and his soulfulness; he would degenerate completely, he would never turn to his inner sense, to the heart of everything, to the soul, nor would he manifest soulfulness. The external form and the visible world would be everything that exists for him. He would stop being a personality, as only a subject who has opened himself to his essence can be a personality, with a soul that enables the invisible and inner to manifest. And that invisible is far more powerful than the visible - it enables it. That is why all things (all of nature) are set so they make man, with their transience and instability, turn to himself, to the soul, to experience suffering when attaching to something outer. Even if we find love in another person, even if it is temporary, it in itself carries the quality of eternity that directs us to our shared inner essence. Everything that is good and valuable in this world comes from soulfulness and carries the divine inspiration with itself, it has eternal value because it points to eternal, transcendental values. That is why in the beginning of his teaching, Buddha said that everything is painful and unstable, and at the end, on our deathbed, we should not seek refuge in anyone, but ourselves.

After this insight into the first truth, the **second truth** is revealed to the objective mind: suffering which is a result of adherence is the cause of its own occurrence. This is the thirst for spontaneous activity in nature, with which it causes action for renewal, and gives birth to new beings with joy and passion; beings who, oblivious to the whole and the final outcome, find their joy here and now, sometimes in individual objects of the relative world, motivated by the lust of their instinctive needs, bound by the illusion of the eternal life of one shape (body), and the illusion of their personal power. This thirst for spontaneous activity in nature springs in humans as the experience of sensory abilities of the body, from identification with the body, and attachment of sensory experiences to the outer foundation of the senses (tanmâtrâ). People are comfortable with their eyes, ears, nose, tongue, body and mind in that attachment; then the thirst occurs. To them, shapes, sounds, smells, tastes, body stimulation and contents of the mind are visible and pleasant; in the attachment to thirst for existence is the cause of all suffering. To people, consciousness which is created by seeing, listening, smelling, tasting, touching and thinking is pleasant; in that attachment, such conditioned consciousness creates an irresistible thirst for conditioned existence. To people, feelings, perceptions, expression of will and states of mind which occur by seeing, listening, smelling, tasting, touching and thinking are pleasant, even though these attachments are the roots of suffering and man's inauthentic life.

The third truth is connected with the second, and says that suffering has its end, possible by ending (transcendence) its causes, by ending the desire for a conditioned existence. The natural passion for its renewal should be ended with purification of consciousness; by abandoning it and giving up on it for good, by completely dissuading oneself from its attracting effect; by making it something that does not concern the unconditioned essence, the soul of man. Wherever adherence to existence in time appears, there it can and must be abandoned and eradicated. The eye, ear, nose, tongue, body and mind are pleasant and cause attachment that can and must be abandoned and eradicated. The alert ones carefully stand at the very entrance of their senses, perceptions and expressions of will for action, and they do not permit themselves to form attachment, for unfavourable influences to enter and prevent them from developing further. Visible shapes, sounds, smells, tastes, body stimulations and the contents of the mind cause attachment that must be done away with. The consciousness that is conditioned with these six sensory areas, as well as feelings, observations, expressions of will, and all the mental states caused by the sensory area, causes an attachment that must be stopped *during its occurrence*. It is not life itself, existence and sensory abilities that are stopped and abandoned, but the blinding and limiting **attachment of consciousness** to them, in order to purify itself for the reflection of the unconditioned divine consciousness that precedes the first condition of manifestation of everything; the being itself, and its senses, only then, in unconditionality, become the perfect mediators, unrestricted openings for the beings to experience the presence of the divine source of existence.

When the necessity of cessation of attachment of consciousness to conditioned existence in time becomes the only certainty, the ***fourth truth*** occurs: there is only one unmistakable path that leads to the cessation of all of inauthentic and transient survival in humiliation, before the element of fate and the creative victory of man's soul overcomes unconscious natural occurrences.

It is an eight-fold road made up of:
- correct understanding
- correct thinking
- correct speech
- correct operation
- correct living
- correct effort
- correct focus of attention (*satipatthâna*)
- correct contemplation (*dhyânam*)

Understanding is correct when the four basic truths of existence presented here are properly comprehended.

Thinking is right when it is deprived of lust (attachment), hatred (repulsion) and misconception (fiction and metaphysics).

Speech is correct when lies, gossip, scolding and chatter are avoided.

Actions are correct when we do not endanger the life of any living being, when we do not take what is not given to us or what is unnecessary, and when we do not cheat anyone.

The correct way of living is the one that enables rectitude in every way.

Correct effort occurs as a desire to avoid bad, unfavourable states, and to overcome those that have already occurred; also in the effort made to encourage useful states that have not yet taken place, and preserving the present ones, bringing them to perfection.

The correct focus of attention (satipatthâna) is the whole-day practice of strengthening the presence of consciousness in the body, feelings, general states of mind and conditions of occurrence of each thought; when it is performed diligently, with a clear understanding and perseverance, with which attachment to the world as well as repulsion towards it is eliminated; or in short when ignorance of the world has become clear.

***

Vipassana and *satipatthâna* is practised in the way described here; insight into reality, all day long, as a way of life, as a way to learn about life, whenever possible but especially when we think it is impossible. The practice then is the most effective.

The focus of attention is the practice that crystallizes and consolidates the purest consciousness of the soul that can ever be possible in this world, while we are in a physical body. It is also known as the consciousness of the Self (atman) or transcendental consciousness of our soul. Its purest presence happens only in the sitting practice of meditation, with absorption or complete focus of consciousness within oneself - known as samadhi. It will be described in the next chapter as rŭpa-dhyânam. These two practices of awareness or awakening are practiced together; rŭpa-dhyânam as the sitting practice of meditation, and satipatthâna as the practice of nurturing the consciousness of oneself in action and in everyday movement and action. In the sitting practice of meditation it is completely experienced within oneself, and in the focus of attention it is applied on oneself during interaction with others in the outer world, in ways the environment and life demand, without choice or imposition.

We become aware of the consciousness of ourselves in ourselves with meditation, and then with the focus of attention we recognize and apply it to the outer world, through the course of events. The more we become aware of ourselves, our Self or the soul, the more we recognize the same consciousness in the outer world, as life itself and existence. Only in this way can it become whole and truly achieved. It cannot be externally achieved if we do not firstly realize it within ourselves, nor can we truly realize it in ourselves as the consciousness of the soul if we do not recognize it and apply it outwardly, as the divine consciousness which enables everything. The more we go towards consciousness of the Self, of our soul, the more that same consciousness of the soul comes closer to us through the dramatic events of life. Everything we experience when we start the practice of meditation will be directed by our Self or soul; there will be numerous temptations of how to recognize consciousness and how to apply it. This is because the microcosm and macrocosm come together in man, existence and awareness of existence.

In the beginning the focus of attention (*vipassana* or *satipatthâna*) requires effort; it becomes complete and mature when we become aware that it is the only path and the only purpose of existence - not only our own existence, but existence in general; when even the slightest forgetfulness and decline into unconsciousness looks like a fall into death and ruin, as the loss of ourselves, as the source of everything evil in this world; when consciousness of the soul in all events becomes the most important thing, not only in our life but in the cosmos; when preserving the awareness of the Self, of the soul in this world, becomes as important as air is to a drowning man. The more we manage to preserve it, the more its significance is revealed, making it easier to keep. The goal is to preserve the clear transcendental consciousness of ourselves or our soul over 24 hours, in dream and reality. Then it will maintain itself without effort, because it will be no different from the consciousness that enables existence. We will never again be able to lose ourselves because the consciousness of our soul, or the Self, is the same consciousness that enables existence, and is no different from it.

VIPASSANA MEDITATION DURING SLEEP

With meditation, as presented here, all dimensions of human being and existence are brought into awareness. But other than meditation, there is something more we can do to make our existence in all dimensions conscious. We enter the higher dimensions (water, fire and air) spontaneously and unconsciously, when we are not in our body - during sleep. We need to learn how to do this consciously, when awake.

We can become aware of entering and exiting the higher dimensions outside of sleep, in the following way: just before sleeping, when you lie down, re-experience everything you did that day, but backwards, neutrally and without judgment - as if watching a silent movie of our activities.

Do the same thing in the morning when you wake up. As soon as you wake up, remember your entire dream, but backwards, and repeat it. Do this before moving, because movement of the body strengthens physical presence and breaks our memory of the dream.

In this way we become equally aware of our activities in reality and in dreams, and we strengthen and connect our consciousness - the consciousness we always have, that is the basis of existence itself. In this way we can practice meditation even during sleep, because there is no special time and special space for meditation. All of existence, and all dimensions, is appropriate for meditation, because meditation is the strengthening of the consciousness which enables existence. Awareness must not be limited. Erasing all boundaries is the key to awareness - that is, to meditation.

With reiteration of consciousness (with recapitulation) during sleep and during wakefulness, we strengthen the consciousness of our soul, because while we are in the higher dimensions during sleep, we get closer to our higher mind, which is our connection with the divine consciousness of our soul. Then, communication between our lower mind, which we use in this world, and the higher mind becomes much stronger. When we apply this meditation in reality and during dreams, we become more aware during sleep; we experience lucid dreams, out-of-body experiences. When we are unaware in the higher dimensions, then we just blindly dream, and the higher mind is forced to turn to us through dreams, symbolically, indirectly, relying on hints. When we are aware in higher dimensions, then we do not need dreams; we have a direct connection with the higher mind and consciousness of the soul.

All of this is nothing but strengthening consciousness of the soul, independently from the body, strengthening the presence of consciousness of the soul in the body in all dimensions, in the physical and in the astral. Only then is meditation complete.

CALMNESS OF THE BODY - HOW TO SIT

The practice of mental calmness is possible only when the body is still. In order for the body to be still, we need discipline and the right environment. Discipline of the body is acquired with the culture of living, and cessation of confrontations with oneself and with the environment - essentially, by living a healthy life.

Stillness of the body is necessary for meditation because with calmness, the body adapts to non-Hertzian frequencies, which are then transferred to the mind. The body and the mind are the same, but reside in different Hertzian frequencies: the body is the reflection of somewhat rougher frequencies, while the mind is of the finer frequencies. The functioning of the mind is fully reflected by the functioning of the body.

In order to calm the mind, it is necessary to first calm the body. Without complete calmness of the body, it is not possible to completely calm the mind. The idea that the mind can reach higher states of consciousness without discipline and stillness of the body is an illusion, one which many people who do not have the discipline for meditation are enslaved to. They even negate the need to calm down the mind, and ask for alternative methods for transcendence. Yes, the mind can reach transcendence in many ways, but calmness is the only direct way that does not rely on inputs from this world. For calmness, we do not need to do anything. This is what confuses the mind that's accustomed to constant activity. It is the opposite of all that the mind does.

When the body is completely calm, then that calmness is conveyed to the mind. The mind cannot remain very active if the body is still. It can, in the beginning, in accordance with the inertia of previous movements - like the rotation of the potter's wheel that continues to turn even after the potter has stopped - but if we remain still with the body, the mind will also eventually calm.

Positions for calming in meditation are shown in these pictures:

Space where people meditation should, if possible, always be the same, in a room away from disturbance and noise. If we do not have such a place, meditation can be practiced outdoors, in a secluded and quiet spot; however, weather conditions may limit this. Meditation can also be practiced with other practitioners, if there are no options for a private space. In the beginning it's good to create the habit of practicing in the same place and at the same time. This will help to settle the practice.

The best position is one where the arms and legs are joined and crossed together. Then the energy of the body is closed in a circle, making the calming easier. When the limbs are spread, then the energy of the body is sent out into the environment. When the legs are crossed together with the arms, then the circle of movement of energy of the body is closed, and consciousness is easily turned to itself and its source.

However, this is not mandatory. Sufficient calmness is easily reached with any of the positions shown above. It is important only for the back to be upright, but relaxed. To accomplish this, envisage you are connected to a line, running from the ceiling to the top of your head. This will give you a naturally upright back.

In order to be centred properly, it is necessary to sway a little bit, slowly left to right, and to gradually slow the swaying so as to feel our true centre, sitting completely upright, and not leaning to one side.

We always initiate calmness of the body with awareness of the whole surface of the body, the skin, from head to toe. We feel the entire body in this way. In everyday life, we are not usually aware of most of our body. So in order to calm it down, we firstly need to become aware of its entire surface.

After making the entire surface of the body conscious, we make breathing conscious. This will be explained in detail in the chapter of the same title. Here, we will only mention that awareness of the breath only serves for the awareness of the body and the cessation of wandering of the mind. It is the method to stop the mind from identifying with its contents and from projecting itself into time. With calmness of the mind, time disappears and only the timeless present remains. This is a simple method to calm the mind without any ideological preconditions.

There are methods of calming the mind with mantras or visualization. We give one shape to the mind, one thought or picture on which to focus, so as not to wander spontaneously through the multitude of thoughts and pictures and become involved in associations or unnecessary analysis, because all of that is not meditation. Such a visualization method may be successful, but the question remains about the meaning or ideology that mantra or picture (*yantra*) represent. It is of crucial significance that the meditation is completely free from any ideology, philosophy or religion. All of that comes from the mind, and the consciousness of the soul does not have any religion or philosophy. The soul is far beyond all of that. Consciousness is at the base of existence itself. Meditation deals with pure consciousness. Meditation and consciousness of the soul do not belong to any religion.

The highlight of calming the body, as a precondition for calmness of the mind, is calmness of the eyes and sight. Movement of the body always follows movement of the mind - the mind is conscious and the unconscious master of the body - but movement of the eyes, sight, is the finest of all body movements and the closest to movement of the mind. That is why when we calm our sight, we also calm the mind. In moving the eyes, all of our activity is reflected.

Therefore, the ultimate goal in calmness of the body, after the skin and the breath have been made conscious, is calmness of the eyes. We calm sight by looking down the nasal line, about one meter ahead of us, in the direction of the floor, but without focusing on any single point. The look should remain diffuse. When the look is focused, then the mind is focused. When the look is diffuse, the mind is unable to be occupied with any contents.

It is important to stay with a calmed body and look for at least one minute to feel the first benefits of meditation. This will motivate you to continue, until you reach 20 minutes of complete stillness of the body and mind. This is the aim of practicing meditation for beginners. This goal is achieved with gradual increases of time, from several minutes in the beginning to twenty minutes for regular practice. Later, an experienced practitioner can sit in meditation for even longer, if it suits him.

It is important to know that for calmness of the mind it is unnecessary, even very harmful, to attach philosophical or religious approaches and preconditions. This is how the mind/ego defends itself; it invents all possible and impossible philosophical and religious reasons for its calmness, that is for further activity. It will invent completely new Cartesian meditation, just to stay active. But there are no mental preconditions for calming the body and the mind.

The mind is calmed with calmness of the body, and in no other way. This is the law, and it must not be overlooked. No one in this world who has not found a way to calm the body can have a calm mind. He will remain deceived in this respect, no matter what spiritual insights he might have had. The ego will give us all the candy from heaven to save itself. The enlightened man is easily recognized by his conscious body, harmonious and well-balanced in movement.

Indeed, calmness is nothing other than the process of mastering by overcoming. If we cannot master and overcome influences of the body, which reflect the rougher aspects of the mind, then we certainly cannot master the mind itself, nor overcome its influences.

Calmness is the condition for any transcendence, for any experience of higher transcendental consciousness. 'Transcendere' means 'to overcome'; in order to be objectively aware of something we need to be above it, we cannot identify with it. This is how the cessation of identification is the condition for awareness of the body. With calmness of the body and the mind we overcome them. *The body and the mind are not active for external reasons, but because we have identified ourselves with the external world. Each activity of the body and the mind is due to an identification. This is why they are not quiet - because we are identified with the contents.* The only reason we can no longer identify with them is because we have discovered something higher and more important than the contents of the mind: consciousness of the soul that enables the mind and the body.

All of the proper conduct and discipline that people learn in this world, in all societies and religions, is but a pale shadow of the discipline of mastering the body in meditation. To a practitioner of meditation, who has mastered his body, no outer discipline is needed, no social norms of behaviour. He is the embodiment of discipline and the physical culture, for the right reasons; not for some religious ideology and social conditioning, but for himself, for the consciousness of his soul which manifests itself in this world through man. Man can act properly only to the extent that he has a connection with consciousness of the soul. Restlessness of the body and the mind are the main obstacles to the manifestation of consciousness of the soul. When the mind is calm, consciousness of the soul is manifested all by itself. It is always there, as the source of existence. We must not disturb and prevent it with our body and mind.

CALMNESS OF THE MIND IN MEDITATION OR CONTEMPLATION (*DHYÂNAM*)

Meditation essentially consists of two parts.

The first part relates to achieving calmness of the mind and the body, until achieving a state of complete transcendence, or *samadhi*. In the Buddhist practice of meditation this is called *rűpa-dhyânam*. It is the phase of transition from Hertzian to non-Hertzian frequencies of consciousness, from the physical world of shapes to the non-physical world of quantum consciousness. This is the phase of achieving pure transcendence, where the objective world disappears, and pure consciousness remains - awareness of oneself is more powerful than it has ever been in the objective world.

Once this is successfully accomplished, with full understanding, what naturally follows is the second phase, which represents returning from that state of consciousness to the world of shapes; the transition from non-Hertzian to Hertzian frequencies of consciousness. This is called *arűpa-dhyânam* in Buddhist practice. More precisely, it is the recognition that both frequencies are two sides of the same coin; there is no duality. The unmanifested divine consciousness of the quantum field is at the base of this manifested world, and this manifested world is no different from its unmanifested foundation, ether or *akasha*, otherwise known as the universal quantum field. According to the teachings of the Buddhist reformer Nagarjuna, at this point shape is void and void is shape, absolute and relative, *samsara* and *nirvana* are one and the same. After all, it is only possible to see the real nature of this world at its base or essence.

When we see the world in this way, not only as manifested and material, but from the highest perspective of the quantum mind, then we see it whole in all dimensions, and nothing is hidden from us. The consciousness of the soul manifests itself, undisturbed, through our being. That is the final state of man's awakening in this world, and also the ultimate goal of meditation.

Rűpa-dhyânam
Four degrees of mental calmness

Meditation is practiced only during intervals of time (unlike the whole-day focus of attention), from twenty minutes to an hour, and in a specific, secluded and appropriate place. It is intensive absorption during which, for a short period of time, complete focus (*samadhi*) of space-time is achieved. It is the moment of man's complete and conscious presence in existence as it is, the moment of the most direct confrontation with it. Only at this moment can the true independence of the soul from all shapes of causative phenomena in time be recognized. So, we realize the independence of a soul when we see the true nature of existence.

In meditation, the being renounces itself during the phase of stillness of the body and mind; more accurately, it renounces its projection on the timeline that constitutes the objective world; it renounces all the contents of temporal phenomena; it renounces the oblivion of itself in order to spare the consciousness of its permeability for the unconditionality of the divine soul.

Consciousness transmits through itself the presence of the divine soul only when it calms, and faces pure being - existence itself - and that happens when it is not projected (avoided or forgotten) over time and space. By doing so it gets itself manifested as the objective world, but it gets focused onto its outcome, and it makes an inward turn to itself, the man's Self during meditation. Then the being becomes transparent and spiritual, it becomes the revived divine consciousness. In the presence of pure consciousness of the soul, the Divine self is directly actualized through existence. Without complete withdrawal, calmness and abstinence from involvement in temporal existence, there can be no objective insight into the true nature of everything, nor creative participation in it.

Contemplation (*dhyânam*) is not so much about achieving something, as it is letting go of the ambition for achievement, and the pure inactivity of the body and the mind, where the body and mind are spontaneously balanced and calmed, removing all opposites and tense unilateralism, and all the sources of suffering. Man in meditation (*dhyânam*) is released for the first time from all ideas and presumptions about the world, about what he is and what he is supposed to be, from himself, from all the tensions and struggles for their realization, and he surrenders to the until then unnoticed but always present perfection of the one who has enabled omnipresence since time immemorial.

The essence of contemplative mindfulness (*samadhi*) is in complete suspension of happenings of the being, and disposing of the heritage of previous experiences (impressions and habits - *samskara* and *vasana*). With that, the reduction of the being to its primordial origins can be achieved, to cleanse him of all the sins of an inauthentic life - the way of life caused by the dynamics of *gunas*, the imbalance which causes instability in all forms of existence. The origin is the primeval state of ideal harmony and balance of its constituting factors (*gunas*). This is the *materia prima* to alchemists. This reduction (the death of "the old man") is necessary for the complete transformation of a being aspiring to spiritual freedom (the birth of a "new man"), because this cannot be performed with the shapes of existence which have already been established through time (John, 10:17-18). They are wrong, and they must be dissolved; on shaky and unbalanced grounds the perfection of the divine consciousness of the soul cannot be maintained.

Samadhi is at the same time man's most authentic Self, which shows that purification, which is the topic here, practically refers to the human being and its own transformation. The human being is a microcosm, which means that the outcome of the cosmos is resolved in it. Therefore, the outcome and the perfection of existence cannot be realized with changes in the world, with science, (religious) metaphysics, nor religious institutionalization, but only with quiet, personal self-realization.

***

Contemplation (meditation) has four degrees.

1. The translation of the original text of Buddha's speech about the first degree of contemplation reads as follows:

The monk, when he turns off sensory tendencies and immoral experiences, stays within the reach of first absorption. That state, followed by imagination and thinking, is born out of solitude, with pleasant feeling of enjoyment. The monk fulfills and permeates the whole body with that pleasant feeling of enjoyment, coming from loneliness, so that no part of his body remains unaffected by that feeling.

The first degree of meditation refers to stillness of the body. By sitting in the upright position for meditation, the body must learn to be absolutely calm and relaxed, without any movement except breathing, for at least half an hour, and one hour at most. In doing so, imagination and thinking which project time are present.

In other words, the experience of the world and personal past is present. Imagination is the memory of previous experiences, the designing of present time and prediction of the future. Thinking is the elaboration of an idea, which does not have to be related to personal experiences.

With calmness, pleasure is born, because of the victory over unconscious movement of the body; this pleasure permeates the entire being. By stopping established habits in movement and behaviour, the vision of the possibility of complete victory over conditionality and time occurs for the first time; being free of illusions of the future and burdens of the past becomes possible. Such insight fills this mindful calmness with excitement and satisfaction.

The feeling of contentment in overcoming the will of the body through discipline is manifested as a pleasant warmth, a tingly sensation in the plexus that permeates the entire body. This sensation, called tapas in ancient times, refers to the waking of energy as a result of a successful ascetic effort. Without it, there could only be the violent stiffness which exhausts the body instead of to inspire the soul in seeking freedom from the body. The ability of a being to be calm is the basic indicator of the intellectual maturity of an integrated personality and presence of unconditioned consciousness of the soul. The divided and intellectually immature personality will not be able to be quiet for a minute. Relaxation of being is a measure of spiritual maturity.

2. The translation of the original text of Buddha's speech about the second degree of contemplation reads as follows:

What is a noble silence? – The monk who has narrowed his imagination and thinking (identification with contents of consciousness) resides in inner calmness, in the focus of the mind, within the reach of the second degree of mindfulness. That state arises from the mindfulness of deprived imagination and thinking, but with a pleasant feeling of satisfaction. That is called a noble silence'... As the lake filled with water that springs in it, and there is no inflow of the water either from east nor from the west, nor from the north nor from the south, so unless the rain falls from the sky from time to time, still in that lake fresh water will flow, power it and fulfill it, so that no part of the lake remains out of reach of fresh water... like that, monk fulfills and pervades the entire body with that pleasant feeling of satisfaction arising from the noble silence, so that no part of the body remains unaffected with that feeling.

The second degree occurs when physical calmness of the body is so easy and effortlessly settled that it, by itself, calms the mind. The body is calm when consciousness is liberated from identification with it, and overcomes it. In the same way thinking is quieted when identification with the mind's contents, with what has been imagined, finally stops; when man recognizes the authenticity of his being that persistently resides consciously in the first degree of contemplation, and based on this realizes the instability and inauthenticity of all past and future life based on thoughts, which constantly shift in linear sequence and so project time; when behind the vortex (*vrtti*) of thoughts man recognizes himself as existence which is timelessly here and now, that always is, and to whom all diverse thoughts appear as transient illusions. **The characteristic of the second degree is the first turn toward mental calmness, the first experience of transcendence of the mind.**

Thoughts originate from non-Hertzian frequencies of ether or *akasha*; they are the finest events of nature, so fine that it seems they are not from nature, but ours, that our thoughts are in our head. But thoughts are not ours, they are just compressed and entwined in us, and that is why we have the ability to remember and repeat them when searching for their meaning. Ours is only the repetition of thoughts, and not the thoughts themselves. Since thoughts group in us, they appear as though they are ours. That is the last illusion with which nature conditions the soul of man. In a way, they are ours, but we did not create them, but merely adopted them to save them from the loss of sense, giving nature final meaning with our soul. When an awakened man thinks and speaks directly from his soul, each thought and word of his is then *logos*, that creates the world; it reveals the meaning of everything, heals all wounds and directly implements the divine energy of life in this world.

When we overcome thoughts by understanding their nature in the light of consciousness of the soul, and we recognize ourselves as the pure consciousness of the soul - only then have we stepped into freedom and awakening. This first step is possible only in meditation, in the second degree of absorption.

This, too, is achieved gradually. Firstly we should turn away from the wandering adherence to a multitude of new contents and ideas, by attaching attention firmly to one thought: "Who am I?" or "Who does the thinking?"

No matter what kind of thought emerges, we should not follow it, nor fight it, but turn attention towards us, here and now, with this question; towards the one who turns thoughts into an inner dialogue, towards the one who is aware of the contents of each thought. The key to success is, therefore, in the realization of this **turn-**

ing away from thoughts, and participation in their contents, ***towards oneself***; no other "achievement," religion or concentration does the trick here. We should not search for the answer to this question, in the same way we should not use it as a mantra, but simply use it to **turn to ourselves**; we are the answer to the question.

Turning attention towards oneself in meditation practically starts with calmness of sight. The eyes are an opening through which the mind perceives the world. That is why the eyes move with the mind, they are the finest sensory organ, and through them we perceive the most. When we completely calm our eyes (for practical reasons, observing a point between the eyes), then our attention is automatically turned backwards, towards the source of the mind, the pure consciousness, and the mind is calmed. When spontaneously left to its own devices, attention moves away from the subject, through the eyes, towards an outer object. When we disable that by calming sight (by looking at a point between the eyes), the energy that spontaneously radiated outward now automatically turns back to its source. Because it cannot stop, the energy is always moving. The same effect is achieved if we meditate with our eyes opened. Then the gaze needs to be lowered and without focus, diffused. While the gaze deals with some shape, the mind becomes engaged. When it does not look at any shape, then the mind does not have anything to deal with, and starts to calm. Calmness of the eyes in meditation is the final act of calming the entire being - with which transcendence occurs. Only then does meditation begin, or true surrender.

This final act will be achieved only when we are mature enough to abandon our personal past, hopes for the future, and convictions about our individuality, and surrender to what enables everything. Namely, everything that connects us with the relative world of ignorance and suffering (*samsara*) is manifested with movement of our psycho-physical being (and the movement of thoughts, the inner dialog, is the finest form of that movement). That is why with its complete calmness, we automatically overcome this. In order to 'free' the soul from illusions of this world to which we are tied through the body, nothing is necessary but calmness of the body.

Achieving transcendence, or the differentiation of the soul and the body, ultimately boils down to the distinction between the mobile and the motionless, the inactive witness and the psycho-mental happening, oneself and everything that happens to us.

The focus of attention to a point between the eyes is only a practical way to return to oneself, to be present in ourselves. Because, the more we are present in ourselves, the more we are free from thoughts. The more we are in our thoughts, the less we are aware of ourselves.

Thoughts can never be stopped by direct means, but we can abandon the area of their happening; they do not have reality all by themselves, but they occur with forgetfulness of self-awareness and identification with their contents. Thoughts are the finest movement of a being from itself to an object (psychic or physical); they are a reflection of the involvement of the subject with objects; they are the result of attachment to the world. That is why thoughts can only be quieted in an indirect manner: by turning to oneself, towards the source of awareness of thoughts and remaining there, in the pure wakefulness which is aware of the one who joins thoughts to semantically connected information, and the thoughts themselves. If we try to calm the thoughts (the mind) in some other way, with meditative control or through an effort of concentration, then we only give them a reality which they themselves do not have, and we create a counter-effect. Then, our I (ego) and the mind are divided into the thought and the one who controls the thought. Thoughts can only be overcome with the realization of their true nature, by becoming aware of the fact that they keep turning around our I (ego), but they are not ours - we do not have to fight against them. We give reality to all thoughts - they do not have reality by themselves. We are never present in ourselves when we are thinking; we are present in ourselves only in the alert silence of the mind.

In meditation we always go behind: behind the eyes, behind each feeling, behind each movement, always towards the one who sees, who thinks, who feels, the one who is conscious. We are behind everything. Behind the entire being and existence. Meditation is always that constant turning behind, in witnessing, and not in finding something.

Only in this way is each new imagining gradually slowed down, suppressed and extinguished; and when only pure consciousness remains, one which is presence and existence, does man come to himself, to the consciousness of his soul.

He is then calm and quiet, because he realizes clearly that thoughts are the burden of the past and the hopes for a better future, the same illusion which causes one to flee from the present, which is eternity and pure unconditionality. The mind is always on the move, in imagination in the past or the future, it can never be present in the present moment, because then its construction of temporal occurrence collapses into an eternity of unconditionality, which the being recognizes as his only reality, always here and now. Therefore, when we are present in the present time, thoughts automatically disappear, and the mind is calm.

Mindfulness of existence in the present, complete presence in oneself in the only reality, is called samadhi. Such timeless mindfulness in reality is experienced by man as his essence, the Self, or authenticity. This is the peak of crystallization of consciousness because the being has come to its outcome; nature finalizes its shapes through time and completely opens the consciousness of our soul as the eternal presence. Hence the peace. After samadhi, nature is shown as the living manifestation of divine consciousness.

The second degree of meditation happens within as inner silence which perceives that although mental activities take place in us, we do not have to participate in their illusions. Even though thoughts happen in us, they are not ours, in the same way that the body does not represent our essence. When we stop identifying ourselves with thoughts, then the noise of thoughts stop, and being slave to a timeline is stopped in the free silence of present time, because of the unity of the one who thinks and the one the thought was meant for during the inner dialogue. The independence of consciousness in the whole affair certainly adds to this.

The silence of awakening in man occurs when he sees there are not two beings or two minds in him, but each activity and each thought is he himself; and by engaging himself in oblivion which results in creation and repetition of the mind's contents, allowing himself to be assimilated with that activity; when he recognizes his power to decide whether he chooses to repeat thoughts and identify with them, escaping into time and dreams, or whether he will remain who he is without them, here and now, and take responsibility for his decisions, ensuring that the situation remains the way he makes it out to be. Therefore, even though our thoughts are not ours, they are by themselves the finest vibrations of the being of nature, vibrations transformed into information; we create and repeat them as if they were ours in the process of identification with objects and oblivion of the fact that consciousness is the only reality. ***Because of that oblivion, our being vibrates in such a way that it keeps repeating thoughts. Only due to the proximity of our soul's consciousness, this repetition is not mechanical, but moves toward meaning.***

The silence in us occurs when we see that everything that happens in the mind, in our entire psyche, is an integral part of being of nature, the same as our organs and the hair on our heads. If we can calm the body by not identifying with it, we can also calm the mind by strengthening independence from it. With strengthening the consciousness of his authenticity, man will realize that he always exists as the key player behind everything: both in activities and in silence, with thoughts and without them. But, consciousness of this is permanently strengthened only with the restraint of activities of the mind, because in this way his freedom from that finest conditioning is proven. Only from the realization of freedom by participating in existence is full responsibility acquired, the power and freedom to participate in all events. By having achieved the state of pure consciousness in meditation, we realize that thoughts also constitute part of the same being. Then, our thoughts bother us no more, they pacify themselves because we have accepted the wholeness of our being. We do not have to design anything, because we have realized existence itself. Then we are relaxed and quiet.

However, realization of oneself as the responsible creator of each physical and mental occurrence provokes repulsion and a need to escape in the face of such responsibility, hence, such occurrence becomes delayed for the future. Then thoughts reappear and that is **why mental tranquility in the second degree lasts for a short time**, because of man's inability to take permanent responsibility for what it brings; leaving only inspiration and excitement for its existential significance. Seeing oneself, even for a moment, as the person responsible for every deed and psychological condition, man immediately escapes back into the safety of old conditionality, into an irresponsible laissez-faire attitude of the old style, depending on external influences and habits. Old habits die hard because they were created over one's entire life experience, nurtured by cultural and religious traditions, which invariably put emphasis on external influences. They should be broken in such a way that we choose to linger in inner silence bravely, despite the noise and beliefs of the whole world.

It is of extreme importance that this moment of knowing oneself in meditation is not converted into a myth, that the memory of it and the impressions of freedom brought by that moment do not become a lie; that we do not delude ourselves that we are still in it, that we have it as our permanent quality. That is how a schizophrenic situation will occur, by thinking that we are aware of ourselves, while in reality we do everything in the same way as unconscious people do. The moment of samadhi is only a moment, but very valuable, and as such, it should be perceived but not deified. We must not make something else out of it. Only when, with enough repetition, we clearly begin to see the difference between that moment and the rest of the time, will we come to realization that, in that timeless moment of samadhi, we are our true nature and salvation, and everything else is just slavery. Only that differentiation will lead us to permanent change.

Therefore, it is extremely important that the first short-lived experiences of samadhi are not mixed with contents of the mind, especially not with the subconscious contents and programs with which the mind is conditioned. Then a very complicated situation arises, which can interfere and divert the process and jeopardize meditation, and even the life path of man. Man becomes a fanatic of half-truths and metaphysical convictions, which may throw him off the scent, and lead him away from the right path. The only right path is to continue the experience of samadhi with the practice of meditation, in the way he did before, to strengthen and purify himself with repetition. Only the pure consciousness of the soul, which is strengthened in this way, can bring the true fruits of meditation. Nothing that comes from the mind can do this. It can only hinder you. Here, we must emphasize once more that meditation is the purification of the consciousness of the soul from everything that the mind imposes and brings. After all, this is only the second phase of meditation. There are four. We should not stop halfway through the process. However, the luring power of samadhi is so great, that the temptation to mix it with the contents of the mind is very big.

Nothing can ennoble and set man free like the silence of the mind reached in the second degree. It fulfills and permeates the entire body with a pleasant feeling of exaltation, satisfaction and realization, which occurs as a result of recognition of freedom from the mind, so that no part of the body remains unaffected by the feeling. Inner silence causes a thrill in man because he then begins to recognize his individual being in holistic unity with the whole universe. Then, the body disappears as a separate whole, resulting in a merging of its individually shaped energy with the energy of the whole, and awareness of that unity permeates it with an enthusiastic bliss. This can be followed by assorted experiences: a powerful chill that permeates the whole body, ecstasy, clarity which grows into never before seen light, whereby the previous experience of the presence of the body disappears, or (if there still are mental contents in deeper layers) it is followed by visions of various deities whose name and shape depend on the cultural background of the man. The body is, during the moments of realization of the second degree, completely calm, as if it were made of rock; but it is also light as if weightless. Movement is made impossible, and breathing is almost imperceptible, because calmness of the breath goes hand in hand with calmness of the mind. The breath is the rougher and the mind the finer form of circulation of the same energy. Such calmness in inner silence is possible only when supporting his Self, man consciously finds independence from the body and mind, independence from all manifested existence in time. This overcoming seems, in terms of the common egoistic experience, as the abandonment of his being and dying, because the body and the mind have unjustly been held captive to his own permanent characteristics. Faced with himself in full awareness, in the second degree of absorption, the entire being stops for a moment, because the big work of its creation has then come to its timeless outcome. The thing which dies is actually the old mind, but without its death, there is no resurrection into the freedom which is life itself for the man.

The individual consciousness of oneself or 'I' is the only thing which we should be made aware of in meditation. 'I' (ego) is actually the outcome of the mind, always behind the mind. In its natural, authentic state, the mind is calm and pure, like a mirror. Its true function is to enable the viewing of all existence. The shapes within it turn into pictures, information, thoughts, although they are only vibrations of the mind, shapes which it currently assumes, like water that assumes the shape of the wave. But we always watch the wave, not the water. That is why we identify with the contents of the mind, because we are unable to distinguish them from the mind itself; we become what we think, the thing we are obsessed with (which ultimately represents psychosis, and in a milder form the everyday life of an average man). We always vibrate in accordance with the vibrations of the mind; that is, thoughts which are not ours, like the dancer who plays to the tune of music which is not his. The goal of meditation is to make the mind still, to stop repeating thoughts, and that means to stop moving (vibrating) in accordance with thoughts, that is, for 'I' to stop moving. **Meditation is the cessation of movement of 'I'.** Hence, it is important to calm the body first. This practically means when 'I', as the awareness of oneself, becomes pure, without movement, i.e. projecting objects which it forgets itself with, it becomes absolutely aware of itself, and in that way it becomes aware of the pure consciousness that enables it, the consciousness of the soul, the absolute outcome of existence; and then it disappears. When an individual, with complete calmness, recognizes its true nature, he or she immediately stops being that individual and becomes in the absolute sense unified with the one that enables everything, with the divine consciousness. That is why man cannot remain the same when he realizes himself. 'I', or the mind, will stop moving, that is, repeating thoughts, then with calmness, he realizes that the attraction towards objects leads him to movement, which, again, is nothing but his thought projections, and that the objects are nothing by themselves. All of nature is one being, so in it, there are no separate and special objects we would aspire to – it is only the mind that creates objects, gives them individuality and characteristics, and then goes towards them. The mind is moving in a closed circle; it itself generates the world of special objects which set it in motion.

From the point of view of meditative practice, this means that all the phases described here need to be experienced in their own 'I' ('I think', 'I breath', 'I am calm and quiet' - it is about a silent and direct experience, and not about one more form of thinking). 'I am' is the other name for awareness in the here and now. The 'I' should become immobile, quiet, composed, conscious of itself and the thoughts it generates with its motion. Then we will become aware of everything that moves as nature, and we will be able to distinguish ourselves from it. **That distinction is the pure consciousness of the soul.** We should be that silence that we experience in meditation, here and now; and not meditate in order to become quiet in the future. The awareness of 'I' is the presence in oneself. The 'I' becomes aware by establishing all the phenomena that manifest through 'I', from moment to moment, without reservation or projecting some new contents. Whenever we project the experience of happening, we are neither aware of our 'I' (self), nor the true nature of that experience, but only of the contents that we have designed. From the pile of these contents the image of the world of an average man is made up, which prevents him from ever seeing the real world. If awareness is not brought properly, meditation will turn into another abstract delusion (which we will call 'meditation').

Everything that happens and that we are aware of and that we testify about, everything that we see and discover, happens with the sole purpose of the crystallization of our 'I', our individual consciousness. That is the meaning of every event. The world does not happen because of itself, but in order to be perceived and envisaged by the conscious subject, our 'I', in order to reach consciousness of the soul, and from there to go back to the divine source, as the consciousness of itself, its manifestation. The divine Absolute through our 'I' perceives the finest aspects of its manifestation. In this is the connection of our 'I' with the creation of everything. That is why with the realization of the true nature of our 'I', we realize our essence, Self or soul, and through it, the divine essence as well.

The direction of this practice is the opposite of all other meditations, which deal with something that 'I' projects, with some idea, notion or vision, with something from (this or that) world. Here, man turns to what creates everything, what projects everything, towards its 'I'; it always goes backwards holding, onto the attitude of testimony, always behind everything, withdrawing into itself, through 'I' to 'Self', to the absolute in self. 'I' is overcome with its realization. We will never overcome it with objectification of its overcoming, or projecting in time, but only by making ourselves (I) conscious of everything. In that way, 'I' will become transparent and it will disappear. It will disappear because it was the other name for wakefulness in here and now. It will disappear so there will be no more our 'I', but it will also become the embodiment of the divine consciousness that enables everything.

This is the way it is because the universe is a hologram; each fragment contains and reflects the whole.

The second degree of absorption in Buddhist meditation corresponds completely to the key description of the purpose of meditation at the beginning of *Yoga Sutra* of Patanjali. It says:

I,2: Yoga is in cessation [blurring particular] »twists in consciousness« (*cittavrtti*).

I,3: [Only] then [in that cessation of particular twists] »the one who sees« (*drastr*) is in accordance with his true nature (*svarupa*).

I,4: Otherwise [»the Man«] is identifying himself with [particular] twists (*vrtti*) [of his personal consciousness, the mind].

This is the breaking point of yoga and Buddhism, and our entire existence.

It is of crucial importance to establish this noble silence in the second degree of absorption (preferably daily), which at first lasts shortly, because even the finest psycho-mental conditionalities, which drag along all the other ones with grave consequences, are abolished during this phase. Their force is too powerful to stop all at once. Everything needs to be done, without delay, in order for the consciousness to be established and gathered in the inner silence, without thoughts of the second degree. When man finds the inner silence in himself once, when he becomes silence, it provides him with the unforgettable testimony that true unconditionality, which enables the existence of everything, is always available, in him, as his freedom. Any further effort means expanding its availability and presence from a personal being towards existence in general.

3. The translation of the original text of the third degree of contemplation reads as follows: *And then, discouraging himself from the feeling of pleasantness, he resides indifferent, attentive and mindful, so he experiences* *with the body that pleasure which enlightened beings express in words: The one who is indifferent and attentive, lives happily. In such a way he resides within the reach of the third absorption'... The same way that in a lake with white, red or blue lotus flowers, some started growing under the water, never coming out to the surface, but they bloom underwater, so the fresh water feeds, fulfills and permeates them from the root to the top of the petals ... in the same manner the monk fulfills and pervades the entire body with that feeling coming from indifferent, focused attention, so that no part of the body remains unaffected by that feeling.*

The third degree arises when the initial excitement due to the calmness of inner unity and silence is overcome, and man resides completely indifferent in it, attentive and composed, without effort and for a longer period; in his true nature, fulfilled with tranquility of inner calmness so that no part of his body remains unaffected by that serenity. In the third degree the experience of transcendental consciousness or samadhi from the second degree increases; the need for escape from responsibility for events decreases, and so does the need for escape from freedom; man starts to adjust to it, more and more feeling it as his true nature. With the process of awareness, we continue to deepen insight into ourselves, and our unconscious contents, stresses, complexes, convictions and implants begin to surface. When we come to them consciously, they are manifested, as if in an explosion. This could be shown as a memory, mental state, emotional reaction or physical sensation or action. It is natural to react to them with adherence, forgetting about inner silence. This is a sign of progress, showing that awareness works and that we are in the process of cleansing ourselves from the inside out.

Progress in the third degree is not only reflected in purification from inner identifications, but also from outer ones. The mindfulness which we acquired in the second degree will be tempted, teased to become involved in different external challenges. All situations and persons who have narrowed our consciousness and made us lose our wakefulness and sobriety are observed from a different angle; they lose their grip over us, we cease to be fascinated by them, and we become more objective regarding them - and therefore, more independent and awake.

By strengthening the experience of inner silence, we gain an increasing distrust towards everything the mind projects and imagines, and we gain trust in the being itself, and its source, the divine which enables it. We can prolong and keep inner silence only to the extent to which we trust the divine consciousness which enables it, during the process of our complete surrender to it. We concern ourselves with thoughts only to the degree of our insecurity in the power of the soul which provides us with existence, and our lack of ability to perceive that existence persists without these thoughts, without our entire psyche, without us, and that the soul decides everything, both about us and about existence. The third phase instills faith in the soul that's infinitely greater than us and our mind, helping us realize that its reality can only be seen with pure consciousness, without the mind.

4. The translation of description of the fourth degree of contemplation reads as follows: *And then the satisfaction and dissatisfaction goes away. When, just like that, joys and sadness disappear, the monk resides in achievement of the fourth absorption. That is the state without satisfaction and dissatisfaction, purified with indifferent atten-*

tion... A man is sitting, wrapped in a white robe from head to toe, so that no part of the body remains untouched by that white robe, and like that, that monk sits fulfilling and pervading the entire body with purity of the heart, so that no part of his body remains untouched by the purity of the heart.

And then, when such serenity matures to a sufficient degree, all states are abandoned, both satisfaction and dissatisfaction, in **the fourth degree** of meditative absorption. Any possibility of a schizoid split has finally been overcome, (not merely regarding thoughts as in the second degree); all previous joys and sorrows vanish, all life experience disappears in a complete merging with the unconditionality which enables all of life. In other words, the soul is completely freed from the influences of the body and the world, and retrieves its authentic consciousness, which is of divine origin. This is the purpose of meditation. Man has then overcome his old personality and his individual experiences; faced with the unconditionality of the wholeness, he becomes completely indifferent towards any shape of individual happening in time. Indifference is the main characteristic of the fourth degree, it is neither positive nor negative, but it is neutrality - a reflection of complete purification in contemplation. That purification pervades and permeates the whole body with enlightenment, so that no part of the body remains unaffected by its freedom. In the fourth degree, the body becomes completely pervaded with freedom of the soul, and subdued to that freedom. The body, with its behaviour, is the only area of expression of spiritual freedom in man. That is why mental calming will not be achieved until consciousness becomes unstable in the body itself, in the first exercise of *satipatthāna*. The only cause of mental activity is the loss of presence in the being, which causes a wandering of the mind from the body and present. (Presence in the being is consciousness that we are not the being, but the soul that enables it.) Our habit to always forget ourselves and the present connects us to thoughts. Whenever the mind is not calm, we should return to the first exercise of focus of attention to the body, and breathing. Only with awareness and mastering the body can we make the mind conscious and overcome it, because the mind is the finest function of the body. The fourth degree is samadhi, focus of attention on the outcome of existence, a conscious presence in the true balance and source of all possibilities of existence - the universal quantum field, ether or *akasha*. Everything arises from this unity and the entire cosmos aspires to its conscious renewal. It only happens to a man who is quiet in samadhi.

The fourth degree is complete silence of the mind. These are only words, intended for those who are completely identified with the mind; that is why they should be uttered by novices learning how to 'calm down the mind'. The mind is impossible to calm, because it is activity itself. Without mental activity, there is no mind. When the first three degrees of absorption are directly experienced, then here, in the fourth degree of complete calmness, reality in which there was no mind is directly observed. It is not some object which can be removed so that it no longer exists, or altered to be calm. We can see that the mind itself is empty; each thought is only empty imagination, all mental contents, which overwhelmed us before, are only an expression of emptiness. They are not even . With the insight that the mind and all its thoughts is emptiness itself, and nothing by itself or for itself, we become of calm mind. Actually, we become calm from attachment to the mind. Then the mind (as its natural function, manas) can think whatever it wants, all mental contents and activities will be empty and meaningless for us. That is because in reality they are. This is the vision of reality, and not its abandonment. This is the only real 'freedom from the mind', the only real 'calmness of the mind'. The only real witnessing and awakening. This is samadhi. Quickly, calmness of the mind is understood only as clear insight into its real nature: it is empty, it does not exist for itself. Everything is just a hologram of the divine whole which is always aware of itself.

In *samadhi*, the spaciousness of time gets condensed. The spaciousness contracts and becomes localized to the body itself, and the 'I' and time also contract and disappear, so that half an hour in meditation feels like a second. With such contraction of existence in pure wakefulness, our existence is transformed and purified from all the deposits of old conditioning in deeds, words and thoughts.

Samadhi is the direct experience of the alchemical transformation of being into a more perfect state. With wakefulness, on a local level, in the area of our body and 'I', we accelerate and contract space-time with which the being, on a global scale and over a longer period of time, achieves perfection under the pulling effect of the divine consciousness. Due to the relativity of being and time, and their mutuality, our local realization is equated with global achievement. We can even say that the global is achieved on the local, or that there is no difference between them.

Failure in meditation is a projection of time and the delay in dealing with oneself, as the principle of freedom in nature; constantly imagining that the ideal of the creative principle is somewhere objectively isolated, as God, or in some 'accomplishment' attainable in the course of time, in the future, or in the past - as if it were not the original and timeless reality itself which enables our being here and now.

The silence of divine unconditionality is always present in us, and in this freedom only existence is voiced. Without that silence in oneself, we would never acquire the ability to hear what is happening, nor without calm can we be aware of any happening.

***

The first degree, therefore, contains the imagining (of various) and reflection (of selected contents), excitement, satisfaction and focus in calming. **The second** is a brief period in which there is no mental activity and there only remains excitement, satisfaction and focus. **The third degree** is deprived of active and short-term excitement and the only thing that remains is peaceful satisfaction and the ability to prolong focus. **The fourth degree** is present permanently, with focus, as indifference due to insight into the true emptiness of the mind itself.

The entire process of meditation is a gradual co-living with the soul and divine consciousness, as our true nature. In the beginning of meditative experiences, we experience pure consciousness of the divine reality through effort and as some extraordinary discovery, bringing ecstasy. Gradually, the excitement decreases and the divine is experienced more and more as that which all of existence rests upon, and existence we begin to experience as our own essence. When this becomes the natural state, which in reality it is, meditative practice is complete. However, it often happens that man stiffens on one of the levels of divine consciousness, and he worships it uncritically as though it were some god. The divine consciousness has no characteristics. It is absolute.

Pure or transcendental consciousness is nothing but consciousness present in itself, beyond thoughts, body, past life experiences and the entire world. Thoughts, the body, experiences and the world are objects, and pure consciousness is the subject itself, without objects. Consciousness is always awareness of something, and pure or transcendental consciousness is awareness for itself, pure wakefulness, the witnessing or sheer presence, and such consciousness is no different from existence itself. The subject, that is the being, wakefully resides within himself as pure existence, directly, without object (world) and time. That state is easy to recognize because it causes bliss, relaxation in the final finding of oneself, our true source.

When we unite consciousness and existence through ourselves, then we give our soul to existence. Meditation means getting used to being in ourselves in this way, directly, undivided and authentically just being, living, completely awake as a subject without any objects, without thoughts, corporeality, past, future or world; awake as the eternal being itself, here and now. Only such existence is conscious and its reality is directly perceived.

The subject exists only in relation to the object. When objects disappear, the subject also disappears and so remains pure, absolute being. Therefore, such meditation is not about enclosing within subjectivity, but about opening towards what enables both the subject and all objects at the same time; the only way to reach it is through the subject, by arriving at its source. (This could be called meditation only conditionally, because the term usually means concentrated absorption in some thought contents. The practice described here refers to sitting by itself in silence, which is called *shikantaza* in Zen).

In the first degree of absorption, man, for the first time in his life, experiences freedom from the instinctive impulse of physical movement, overcoming it with his calmness. In the second degree man realizes for the first time that he is not the mind and that he can be free from his determinations and contents, that he can be a separate and independent witness of each thought and psychic experience. Even though it is of crucial importance, this degree lasts for a short time; due to immaturity, this state of witnessing is followed by earlier experiences, frustrations and contents which are beginning to surface as a result of him becoming aware, so that the independence of witnessing quickly disappears. He cannot be free and conditioned with old habits of individual experience at the same time. The third degree is characterized by the disengaging of human consciousness from personal conditionality, personal past; the overcoming of 'I', the assimilation of what has been personal into the free and super personal, into the absolute. The fourth degree is a victory of the soul over the self-will of the body and the mind, and complete indifference towards them, as a permanent state.

All four degrees are characterized by increasing awakening of bliss, because in the process the body and mind are not rejected, but they mature to their natural purpose and blossom; they become the embodiment of the freedom which enables the world itself. It is the process of giving the soul and meaning to existence itself and life as well.

By perfecting all four degrees of *rūpa-dhyânam*, we achieve the perfection of satipatthâna. Only then can we clearly and perpetually realize the transcendental nature of our soul, which is the divine consciousness in us. The fact that we can be completely aware of our body and master it shows us that we are not the body, we are above it. The fact that we can be completely aware of our feelings and independent from their influences shows that we are not these feelings, that we are above them. The fact that we are aware of all the states of mind shows that we do not have to be identified with the states of mind, that we are above them. And the fact that we can be aware of each thought shows us clearly that we are not a single thought, nor are we the one who designs and repeats thoughts (ego), because we can also be aware of this.

All of this is manifested nature acting as the mirror of the divine consciousness of itself, which we ourselves are.

This is the goal and the purpose of meditation and all real spiritual disciplines in general: differentiation of consciousness, witnessing, realization that we are different and independent (*kaivalyam*) from all these modifications of nature or *prakrti*.

SIDDHI - POWERS

CONSEQUENCES OF MEDITATION

When consciousness is focused, purified and cleared in meditation (*dhyânam*) for the smooth manifestation of consciousness of the soul, its power of creation in nature - although grand before - becomes much bigger, and is completely realized. The consciousness now illuminates the being in all dimensions, not just from the field of physical senses. This is why it becomes active in all dimensions, not only in this physical reality. The closer our individual consciousness is, with its purification and calmness, to the principle of unconditionality of the divine consciousness, the greater its creative potential is – and the lesser the modification of existence's restraining hold over it.

Referring to physics, with successful meditation man goes beyond manifested nature and enters its unmanifested area - from Hertzian to non-Hertzian frequencies. This is the area of the quantum field, the cosmic hologram, complete timeless unity, ether or *akasha*. With successful meditation, consciousness has reached its purest state, its original state, and because there is no multitude of consciousness but only one and the same divine consciousness coming to its original pure state, the consciousness of man is recognized as the divine consciousness.

Then the individual consciousness is united with the essence of nature, with the quantum field, ether, *akasha*, divine matrix, holographic universe, dark matter, non-Hertzian spherical energy... there are many names for it. From this essence springs all life energy. In this essence all the causes and consequences of absolutely everything that has ever been manifested or will ever manifest co-exist together, outside of time. When an individual consciousness comes into contact with this field, it becomes the creative consciousness; it can freely use all the possibilities of being, it can act in all dimensions, not just in the body and the physical world. Additionally, it can act in parallel realities, according to which everything exists, and independently from space and time.

Such power of action is here, in the physical three-dimensional world, but seen as 'supernatural' powers (*siddhi*). The powers or siddhi are nothing but the use of non-Hertzian, stationary frequencies in the three-dimensional world, where the Hertzian ones usually rule, a transversal-vector form. Consciousness unifies the frequencies, and is pure enough to be able to reach the foundations of nature (*akasha*). *Siddhi* is the conscious manifestation of the essential possibilities of nature. Consciousness of unity uses nature on the finest level, in its quantum unity. The completely conscious soul of man can use all the possibilities of nature, all of its dimensions. Nature becomes obedient to the soul of man after that soul has become completely aware. That is siddhi. The complete microcosm (an awakened man) automatically sees the cosmos as wholeness, with endless potential.

Patanjali in the *Yoga Sutras* denotes the fruits of meditation with the term samyama. It arises as the sum of all previously achieved disciplines of meditation: *dharana, dhyana* and *samadhi* all constitute *samyama*.

Patanjali literally says:

III, I: Fixing [the entire] »power of detection« (mind-*citta*) to [exclusively] one place [represents] »focus« (*dharana*).

III, 2: When in this [»focus«] is established »the continuous identification« (*ekatanata*) with [chosen] object of attention, [that is called, with technical term] - »contemplation« (*dhyana*)

III, 3: When contemplation disappears, so to say, in the form that is specific for it (*svarupa*) [namely, when this does not represent the effort of the subject to follow the meaning that radiates from the object] and only this radiation of the meaning (*arthamatranirbhasa*) remains [that is called, with technical term] - »unity« (*samadhi*).

III, 4: These three [last »members«] taken together [are called, with technical term] »[superior] summation« (*samyama*).

III, 5: [Only] on achieving this [summations, occurs] the light of Knowledge.

Samyama is no longer the discipline, but the balance that is achieved when the subject and object disappear. *Samyama* is calmness, when there is no more duality inside man and he is not divided; when he becomes one with consciousness of the soul.

The entire process consists of turning inwards, towards his source, towards consciousness of the soul.

The first five steps - *yama, niyama, asana, pranayama, pratyahara* - help man to go deep into himself, beyond the body. The body is the first periphery, the first concentric circle of existence. The second step is to go beyond the mind. Three inner steps, *dharana, dhyana, samadhi*, go beyond the mind. Behind the body and behind the mind is the higher mind, which is the connection with consciousness of the soul, with the source of existence. The centre of being or existence Patanjali calls '*samadhi* without a germ', or 'without a seed' - *samadhi-kaivalya*. This is his other term for facing the consciousness of the soul, the divine consciousness.

Therefore the entire process may be divided into three parts: how to transcend the body; how to transcend the mind; how to surrender to one's own essence, the divine consciousness.

Patanjali's *samyama* is not a concept found in ordinary practice. It is the concept of blooming, helping and allowing what is hidden within us to be manifested.

Practically speaking, in order to bring us closer to the experience of samyama (even though it overcomes any ordinary experience), we can say that it is the consciousness with which we directly perceive existence as pure energy. And energy as consciousness. And both together, as our essence, as the divine presence. That is the consciousness with which we see that there is only one 'divine particle,' which is currently manifested as everything in existence, which is energy itself, which is manifested as matter and phenomena, and which is manipulated by consciousness or intention. To see the 'divine particle' in action with the mind is virtually impossible; we need the help of consciousness that is beyond the mind. That is why we needed the discipline of meditation. No one, unless they became acquainted with the discipline of meditation, can see the 'divine particle' as reality in action. For all those who are identified with the mind, it is only an abstract theory. The idea of it cannot stick in the mind for more than a few moments, before it evaporates.

Only when we permanently become aware of 'the divine particle' in action, when we can see it, are we aligned with the divine consciousness of our soul; only with it can we see the divine reality. Only then can we act in accordance with it; more accurately, only then can it act through us.

This action is what an ordinary mind bound by the body perceives as 'supernatural abilities' or 'powers' (*siddhi*).

There are two phases of the conscious use of all powers of existence: mature and immature.

Immature use is when a conscious subject (person) discovers the universal quantum field for the first time, with all its possibilities, and starts to get to know them, and consequently manifests them in this world.

The mature phase is when all the powers of consciousness of the soul are used for one sole goal: actualization of the divine consciousness, here and now, and the final awakening.

Owing to meditation, we have learned that we can exist without thoughts; we are not the mind but pure consciousness of existence. The mind narrows consciousness of existence and conditions it to fit its own contents. When we learn to be conscious without thought, pure consciousness only, and we exist as being itself, then we are awake and present in ourselves throughout all events, both in reality and in dreams. Only in this way can we be conscious in higher dimensions. That is why the first fruit (siddhi) of pure consciousness is the appearance of lucid dreams and out-of-body experiences. They are the key hint of the final independence of the soul from the body and this world. Without this, its independence would not be actualized in man's experience; or the spiritual preparation for it would be needed until the end of the physical body. It is much wiser to speed up the process, which is otherwise inevitable, by empowering consciousness through meditation (*satipatthâna* and *dhyâna*), and prompting out-of-body experiences. It is better to experience all of this within the controlled conditions of meditation, rather than wait for death to teach us. Since it provides us with insight and prepares us for the big awakening, this fruit of meditation arrives according to importance. When through out-of-body experiences we get confirmation that we are not our body, when through lucid dreams we understand the astral and higher dimensions, then everything else that remains to be discovered become merely fragments.

The special nature of out-of-body experiences or astral projections in higher dimensions is thanks to the fact that we are closer to our higher mind and consciousness of the soul during these experiences. When we come close to them and get to know the higher dimensions, that closeness and experience strengthens communication and understanding of the physical mind for all the influences it receives from the higher mind and consciousness of the soul. With out-of-body experiences and acquaintance with higher dimensions, all obstacles are removed, and the channels for comprehending the influence that consciousness of the soul has on the physical mind are purified.

It is not necessary to do anything special when out-of-body experiences happen. It is enough to develop attention in the astral, to examine all properties of the astral world and to rise up with one's own will, to fly straight up. Then we will return to the body, but we will also experience something of the presence of consciousness from the higher dimensions. This is enough. This will indirectly influence the consciousness of the physical mind, to open itself even more to the higher dimensions. If we aspired to do anything in the astral, hoping to achieve some goal other than making ourselves aware of the nature of that state, it would be magic. However, magic is the action of the lower mind intent on exploiting the higher dimensions. Various short-lived effects and benefits that the mind considers valuable can be achieved in this way, but everything that is done to serve the interest of the lower mind is conditioned by the chain of causality, meaning the creation of further karma, further connection and conditioning of the mind. This is why all magic is negative. It is a big temptation not to use the experience of higher dimensions to strengthen the mind and ego, but for their transcendence, i.e., understanding from higher perspective.

All other abilities of consciousness (*siddhi*) are of secondary importance, and are reduced to exhibitions and manipulations of parallel realities. They can be practiced in the astral body, and then such acquired experience can be transferred to the physical plane. It is possible to practice crossing over from the physical body to the energetic body, and to observe events in the physical world from afar - seeing and hearing through physical obstacles and practicing remote viewing; transforming physical elements at will;[13] beating earth's gravity and flying into space. Traveling across the cosmos is possible with the energetic body, because one moves in the higher dimensions where space-time is compressed; on this journey one is able to actually enter a state of compression of the higher dimensions; it is possible to see past lives.

All of this is possible largely due to the fact that the universe is a hologram and that all the possible realities,

---

[13] The transformation of elements belongs to the same ability of consciousness that controls transformation of other forms of existence, such as habits and behaviour, from thought to technique. Since elements of nature transform constantly, the action of consciousness to change them is only an alchemical suppression of time in this process.

all manifestations, exist in parallel in relative time, that is, timelessly.

Moving objects, or telekinesis, using only the intention of consciousness to connect two parallel possibilities and reality, is quite real - because an object can be everywhere within the quantum field. Actually, it is already potentially everywhere, and the conscious subject is the factor that has the power to decide where it will be observed; that is, where its position can be actualized in the rough physical reality. On the physical plane it appears to us that the object moves from point A to point B. The meditant who performs the siddhi of telekinesis actually sees that it is already in the other place, and he just consciously connects the two realities: the reality where the object is in the first location, with the reality where the object is in the other location. He does not nurture suspicion as to whether this is possible; he only performs this as a being fully aware of the quantum field, in which all realities are already present in the implicit order.[14]

The power of telepathy is nothing but establishing a connection with the quantum field, in which everything is already interconnected in one information field, where the finest vibrations of nature exist, and where all possible thoughts are present. All possible events are also collected as one, before being manifested in different parallel realities, and the power of clairvoyance is nothing but consciously tapping into that field. This is why it is possible to see when and how events will be manifested.

The power of levitation is actually the quality of complete independence from all gravitational forces, a

---

[14] Consciousness of the quantum field and parallel realities are at the base of the speech Jesus gave about powers: we can walk on water if we do not doubt, and we can move a mountain if we have faith.

complete autonomy of the soul that includes the entire body. This is an indicator of superiority of consciousness of the soul over the body. Like when we take some object and lift it up, in the same way the consciousness of the soul can overpower the body completely, and lift it off the ground. Hertzian frequencies of the mind, that are related to time and space, then have to be completely annihilated and turned into non-Hertzian frequencies, into the consciousness of timeless presence and complete self-sufficiency of the being. When the body levitates it releases energy resembling the electrical energy of ball lightning. *In levitation, the energetic aura of the body, with conscious attention, is turned into a powerful electrostatic field - so powerful that it becomes independent from all the influences of nature, independent of the earth's gravity, to such a degree that it can overcome it.* The beginning of this energetic independence was in the act of turning the attention from the object in *dharana* to the Self, towards the source of consciousness, towards the one who is aware. This is the beginning of meditation. A part of this is the turning away from attachment to the senses, away from ties to the contents of the mind, abandoning everything wrong and faulty; that is, everything that had a hold over us, in unconsciousness and conditionality. The perfecting of meditation yields such results. Levitation is only a physical confirmation of the independence of the soul and its unconditionality from the attractive forces of nature. Levitation is the confirmation of autonomy of the soul of man, physically manifested through an autonomous electrostatic field. The earth's gravity pulls us in the same way that unconscious identification with the body and contents of the mind pull us, as a result of oblivion of consciousness of the soul. By awakening consciousness of the soul, man becomes independent from the world, to such an extent that he can fly.

Gravity is an electrostatic phenomenon of large proportions. All bodies affect one another electrostatically and this is gravity; a bigger and more powerful body interacts and bonds with a smaller and weaker one. That is why the Earth holds us with its gravity. Gravity is partly what keeps us here on Earth, but also what defines the conditions of life and everything we get to experience as physical laws, and the drama of life. When we manage to make the autonomy of our soul conscious, and when with consciousness of all dimensions of existence we actualize the independence of our consciousness of the soul in our physical body, with awareness of all the dimensions, then we can with that consciousness have a superior impact on the body, and the attractive power of the earth too.

In other words, all of this is possible only when consciousness in the body, through meditation, completely overcomes the attractive force of Hertzian waves and acquires complete control of non-Hertzian frequencies of the quantum field. In levitation, what happens is that the **electrostatic field of energy of the body becomes harmonized with the frequencies of the universal quantum field or ether.** That is why we said that siddhi is actually the physics of ether in the physical world, or the activity of a quantum mind in a physical body. The quantum field is *akasha*, and *akasha* means space. This is the space in which all bodies levitate. We are already levitating, together with Earth, sun, all the planets and the stars. Everything levitates in the same way in the quantum field, that is *akasha* or ether. When our individual consciousness becomes cosmic, overpowering the lure of the body and the senses, when it becomes one with the quantum consciousness (which it is always, because no multitude of consciousness exists), then levitation of our own body is just the external evidence of that consciousness. With the quantum mind we actualize the reality where everything that exists already levitates, in the divine consciousness of the Absolute. This is achieved when we change the paradigms of our mind, treating it as if it were just a small conditioned subject, until we open up for the divine consciousness which enables everything, and which is us once our mind awakens. It was powerless only while it was sleeping. Then we can, with our intention, affect the manifestation of consciousness in existence, and that manifestation is energy. We can transform the energy of our body, its aura, into a self-sufficient whole, and this in the language of physics means that we turn it into an electrostatic field which becomes autonomous and independent from gravity.

If we can apply this to our body, we can also do so to other bodies nearby, and to external objects. In order to be able to act on energy from the outside, firstly we need to master it in ourselves. Everything is resolved in us. On the outside, we only manifest what we have achieved in ourselves. When we affect the energy or aura of another body, to become a closed electrostatic field, we can move inside whenever we like, independently from gravitation and their will, and this is then called telekinesis.[15] For

---

[15] The extent to which all of this is possible shows us nature. It was recently discovered that many insects fly exactly in the way described here; they levitate by creating strong electrostatic power using their wings. The wings of some beetles that can fly contain tiny chambers that are designed in such a way that through their rapid vibrations (which are also manifested as sound) they create electrostatic fields around their body, enabling them to fly and steer, using their wings. They do not use wings in the way that birds do, by sup-

such action imagination and intention are enough, united with consciousness that includes all dimensions and *akasha*. This is not so much imagination as it is consciousness of the present moment and the complete overcoming of time. The disappearance of time is the consciousness of *akasha* or ether, meaning the quantum consciousness, and something that happens in meditation, in complete focus, in *samadhi*. Our energy field or aura becomes electrostatic, self-sufficient and therefore independent from gravity only with consciousness of the quantum field, the timeless consciousness of *samadhi*, once we realize this as a permanent state of mind, always available.

The mature phase of using the powers of existence occurs very quickly after the immature phase, if everything goes according to plan. Advanced and mature souls pass more quickly to the mature phase, and immature ones more slowly - they are more fascinated with all the possibilities of existence. The mature ones perceive more quickly that there is nothing new, that the only new quality is their wakefulness in the thing that always is, and that wakefulness is the most important; realizing that all possibilities of existence depend on the wakefulness of the soul of man while he is still in existence, his authentic presence in existence. Because nature, without the presence of the soul, is solely an unconscious element. Nothing in nature has consciousness all by itself; some shapes of nature are already sufficiently subtle to absorb and re-

---

pressing the air, but by creating the necessary frequencies. Bees and bumblebees do this since they have disproportionately small wings in relation to their body. Having this in mind, any insect of this kind is evidence of an intelligent design, proving there is superior consciousness at the base of existence, and overthrowing Darwinist materialistic evolution as nonsense.

flect consciousness of the soul, which also comes from the divine consciousness.

The mature phase culminates with insight into the chain of causation in the process of the consciousness of the soul sinking into unconsciousness of existence, and with this it brings the final awakening to the true power of the soul.

When consciousness in meditation is completely composed, purified and cleaned, man sees that the whole chain of causation of existence, the attachment of the soul to the body and matter, consists of twelve hoops:

1. Due to the *ignorance* of unconditionality of the divine consciousness,[16] as the first condition of existence itself, unconscious reactions to events spontaneously occur.
2. Spontaneous and **unconscious reactions** (of samskara) induce the conscious experiences of the average man.
3. Such conditioned consciousness induces his *mind* (identity) *and bodily shape*.
4. Body and mind undergo the *experience of six sensory areas*.
5. One sensory area is based on *touch with subjects and objects* (perception).
6. Touch causes *feeling*, and
7. Feeling causes the *thirst for life*.
8. The thirst causes *attachment* to the renewal of experiences of living.

---

[16] Here, ignorance, or *avidya*, is the pre-planned oblivion of the consciousness of itself, which arises with incarnation in the physical body.

9. This adherence and attachment for the renewal of sensory experiences creates **the illusion** of existence in reality.

10. The illusion of **real and permanent survival** in sensory and physical form causes

11. A new **birth** which leads only to

12. **Old age and death**, into the decay of everything that arises.

With the disappearance of ignorance and unconsciousness in completely purified consciousness of the divine reality, all unconscious reactions which further create conditioned existence and this entire chain of consequences of inauthentic existence for the soul disappears - the chain which ties the soul to the body and suffering in life's drama. *All of this stops when unconscious reactions are suspended consciously, when a person remains still and focused on clear insight into the nature of events.* Our entire existence, up to this moment, was based on unconscious reactions; they were the chains of our slavery. These chains had two kinds of links: adherence and repulsion (desire and hatred). Both brought bad results and suffering. Achieving the level of awareness a witness has or the level of transcendental consciousness, we do not give up on events, in the way it may seem to an inexperienced critic, but we give up on our unconscious reactions regarding those events and, in doing so, we achieve psychological objectivity towards the events in question; avoiding reacting spontaneously we can see reality for what it really is, and then act in an appropriate manner. *When we see events for what they really are, we return the awareness of them directly to the divine through our soul; hence, we then act with the divine consciousness.*

Upon such acting the purpose of the soul in this world is fulfilled. The cycle of the incarnations of the soul stops.

Also, the events which bind us stop repeating. Everything happens because of our witnessing; we are, as a soul, a conscious subject of any event. When we become aware of this, then events stop repeating and things develop in new directions. Everything that shackles us and causes suffering repeats, because we refuse to accept our responsibility; the fact that they happen to us, that they happen because of us, is because of our witnessing, awareness in progress. When we become aware of and accept full responsibility for events, that we are the conscious subjects of each event, then the purpose of each event is realized and they stop repeating. With such awareness we stop being hampered and stuck in unfavourable situations. With such awareness, we create our life and set ourselves free from suffering.

In order to see events as they truly are and to act properly, we cannot rely on 'God's commandments', religion, morality or ethics, reason or logic, knowledge or science, political or economical coercion. Only with transcendental consciousness of the soul can we act properly; without it we always react unconsciously.

How and why does consciousness of the soul bring righteousness to our conduct? With transcendental consciousness of the soul we perceive all the higher dimensions, from which we ourselves are made, as well as existence itself. In higher dimensions, the divisions and differences between all phenomena and beings disappear, while in the highest, ether or *akasha*, all of them become the timeless one. This practically means that when we become conscious of higher dimensions, by entering them via out-of-body experiences or astral projection, we perceive more clearly our union with all of existence, we strengthen our empathy, we perceive more clearly how other beings feel when we influence them. Then it becomes impossible to act violently or to hurt others. This is the concrete reason why consciousness of the soul brings proper functioning and understanding. This happens with the openness of our mind to higher dimensions, and because of the nature of those higher dimensions. From the holistic unity of higher dimensions, the basic ethical principle emerges, which is: do unto others as you would have them do unto you.

Goodness, love, understanding occur only because of contact between the mind and the higher dimensions, where everything is connected in unison. That unity of the higher dimensions in us creates empathy and understanding. All of this brings awareness of the nature of higher dimensions to us.

Without the experience of pure consciousness, we cannot act at all; neither have we ever acted. All our (re)actions were natural action, an integral part of nature, from our thoughts, words, dreams and yesterday's work; like leaves in the wind and the Earth moving around the sun with the other planets.[17] In merging our individual consciousness with consciousness of the soul, we see that all psychophysical activities we have ever done were not done by ourselves, but were been done unconsciously and with the attractive influence of some entity or external influence; and consciously they can be performed only

---

[17] The science of astrology shows us how the natural whole makes us and conditions our movement through life. Only with experience of transcendence can we overcome fate and acquire free will, not as ours, meaning our ego, but as the will of freedom that enables everything, the free will of the divine soul. See my book "Metaphysics of Astrology: Why Astrology Works" for details on this topic.

with the attractive influence of pure consciousness of the soul, which is our essence.

The attractive effect of consciousness of the soul is the greatest power or siddhi a meditant can manifest. This is known as the 'Law of Attraction'. He simply acts from the non-Hertzian consciousness of the quantum field, or pure consciousness. From there, the meditant acts with the intention of creating reality from the higher, quantum level, from the highest dimension, ether, in which all possible realities already exist in parallel; or, better to say, timelessly. Therefore, he with an idea chooses one reality from all the possibilities and empowers it with imagination until it is realized on the physical plane. More accurately, he places it in a certain time and space. Acting with pure intention to create the desired reality is the highest *siddhi*.

All the powers of consciousness of the soul or siddhi are based on understanding the balance between the power of divine consciousness and the power of nature itself, which is about knowing how much we must and how much we can act with the power of our body and mind, using the initiative of our ego, and how much we need to surrender to the power of a higher force, the divine power and will. That is the fundamental problem of people in this world: when and how much do we act with our own will, and how much is the will of the divine power. What share is ours, and what is God's? When and how to surrender to the action of a higher force, how to make it act, how to act together with it, and how to understand it and not to disturb it when it acts? When a person perceives higher dimensions of existence and principles of action through them, the law of realization or materialization,[18] then it is easy to recognize where the boundaries of the mind are, and where and how the higher power of the soul acts. Otherwise, the manual for understanding all these details, the relationships between the lower and the higher mind and consciousness of the soul in action, is *I Ching* or the Book of Change.

Achieving this balance is the topic of maturity of each man individually, but also mankind as a whole. Every child matures from a stage of commitment and expectation that a higher power, shaped as caregiving parents, will provide him with everything he needs. This is a time of carelessness. The child matures by gradually learning to act on his own and take things into his own hands. He should not only expect to get what he needs, but also to create what is necessary by himself. This is the same path all of mankind must walk. Its early and immature phase was religious commitment to a higher divine power that ensures everything, and the mature phase will be people learning by themselves to create the perfect life, the life they need. The divine always ensured everything in the early phase, it was always there, but the mature phase shows that the divine acts directly through man, through his conscious understanding and training. The perfect social order will be the highest siddhi people can manifest.

Only by understanding both sides, the balance of action and non-action, can wisdom be attained; by accepting the higher force and the power of personal action. The true power of man is in that wisdom and balance, and not in emphasizing one side at the expense of the

---

[18] For details of this process, see my book: "The Process of Realization: A Detailed Description of the Process of Every Kind of Realization, the Law of Attraction, from Quantum Fields and the Mind, to Matter."

other (that the ego and mind should have an advantage over higher force, or vice versa). Therefore, man is the most powerful when his mind and body are acting in accordance with consciousness of the soul, as its tool for action in this world.

However, apart from this wisdom and balance, there is an even greater wisdom, and that is in the overcoming of imbalances, which occur wherever any problems exist.

Only with transcendental consciousness of the soul in this world, are we born into the body and truly begin to exist. Until then only nature existed, and it did everything in a spontaneous, conditioned manner – through the body, feelings and thoughts, which are its products, and which we mistook for ours. All our suffering occurred because of this identification with nature, because of the oblivion of the soul, but also because of misunderstanding nature itself. Actually, we do not have power and consciousness of our soul to the point where we are not aware of nature and the reality of this world. By rejecting anything from this world, we reject and distort consciousness of the soul, the divine consciousness. Therefore, there is no greater siddhi than the ability to understand this world. The understanding of the true nature of this world is equal to understanding the divine consciousness.

Of all the fruits of meditative purification of consciousness, the best is that which finalizes the maturing process, providing complete insight into the four basic truths and the chain of causality of existence. Man is awakened from the unconscious survival that characterizes all natural creations with the help of this maturity.

The power of liberation and realization of the authenticity of the soul in this world is the greatest power that a person can manifest.

Buddha differentiated this mature, second phase of manifestation of the power of the soul, when speaking about *arűpa-dhyânam*.

FIVE DEGREES OF ACTUALIZATION OF THE DIVINE CONSCIOUSNESS IN EXISTENCE

Arŭpa-dhyânam

The achievement of pure transcendental consciousness of the divine Absolute in oneself, *samadhi*, is not the end of meditation. Such consciousness needs to be recognized and actualized as existence itself - which essentially it is.

Rŭpa-dhyânam is the entrance into a state of deep meditation and achievement of *samadhi* - pure, transcendental consciousness of the soul. It required discipline.

Arŭpa-dhyânam occurs spontaneously after leaving a state of deep meditation and returning to the world of activity. Arŭpa-dhyânam explains the consequences which occur when consciousness of the soul is brought into the body and into this world, in the reality of our everyday lives.

Buddha devoted his The Shorter Discourses on Voidness (*Culasunnata sutta*) to those who have successfully practiced meditation; he left signs for people to recognize that they are on the right path, to recognize the consequences of meditation with ease. This entire chapter on *arŭpa-dhyânam* is based on this speech.

Until now, in various ways (*rŭpa*) shaped the absorption (*dhyânam*) during a special practice. It was done in the body and the mind, with their restraint and stillness. Up to this point the observer, who is the witness, was crystallized as pure consciousness of the soul. *Arŭpa-dhyânam* is related to the contemplative recognition that is independent from the body and from any exercise that deals with the body or mind. It cannot be shaped (*arŭpa*), but comes of its own accord, as the fruit of shaping. The affirmation of the witness starts here - the soul in existence itself - and in this way existence reveals itself as divine. For the soul cannot manifest itself in any other way, anywhere other than in the real world, the divine world.

Relying on the language of physics, the absorption was formed (*rūpa-dhyânam*) in the physical body in this three-dimensional world, in which Hertzian, transversal vector forms of existence rule. When such meditation is successfully realized, *arūpa-dhyânam* comes spontaneously - as the actualization and affirmation of the purified consciousness of the soul from the field of pure being, from unmanifested nature, the quantum field, *akasha*, non-Hertzian stationary frequencies of existence – into the Hertzian area of the physical world, manifested existence. When pure consciousness of the soul is realized here, it is automatically harmonized and unified with the unity of nature on its finest level, *akasha*. Because of the static, spherical nature of the scalar frequencies of *akasha*, or the essence of nature, it is experienced in meditative absorption (*samadhi*) as complete peace (*nirvana*), fully and completely. The experience of samadhi is explained by the physics of the ether, and by its stationary, scalar characteristics.

Intensive absorption during meditation (*dhyânam*) is related to the constant presence of consciousness in all events (*satipatthâna*) - like the resistance a foot exerts against the ground while walking. Without the occasional resistance against the ground (one hour of meditation for the sake of reflection), the walking part (all day long wakefulness, *vipassana*) would not be possible. In *rūpa-dhyânam*, man comes to unconditionality as the fundamental outcome of all creations, and also the consciousness that perceives them; but such consciousness and freedom from all creations cannot be kept in perpetuity because different happenings of the body, feelings and mental states, interfere with their dynamics. That is why it is necessary that with satipatthâna all these happenings are mutually discerned and perceived as they really are, in all dimensions and shapes, in the body, feelings, states of mind and thoughts, so that they do not have a conditioning and deceptive effect on wakefulness.

Through discernment of all these states we achieve the final insight that we, in our unconscious state, enable all the events of the body, all feelings and mental states. In the completely conscious state, identification with events stops and the chain of karmic causation is interrupted. That is why we can overcome all the states of being and the mind with the awareness that we are not it. That is why the essence of consciousness and wakefulness is the insight that alerts us to the truth of "that is not mine, that is not me". That is why all the boundaries of what is external and internal get erased at this point.

Practically speaking, the non-Hertzian state of conscious, of *akasha*, acts when we are completely calm and in the state of samadhi. When we vibrate, we fall more and more into Hertzian states; this happens in thoughts initially, in the form of the finest vibrations, and then in rougher and rougher ones, down to physical movement.

Complete cognition comes when we combine all these experiences, from Hertzian activities in the rough physical world to non-Hertzian calmness in the quantum field of samadhi. Only then do we realize that we are, in all those cases, equally present as consciousness of the soul, as the divine consciousness that enables everything. In this way, we discover our unity with the divine Absolute.

In *arűpa-dhyânam*, the same unconditionality that enables everything, that is perceived in inner silence of oneself, in *samadhi*, is recognized on the outside, in everything and in each action. The internal becomes external, and vice versa. Having reached himself, the conscious subject becomes objective to such a degree that external and internal, calmness and movement of everything, displays itself as one and the same; he then recognizes the peace of his Self as the essence or soul, in everything that exists, in all of nature and each movement and deed.

This is all a description of the harmonization and unification of consciousness of the soul with the essence of nature or existence. **Man's soul cannot actualize in any way other than through unification with the essence of existence (akasha); nor can the essence of existence be actualized except through the soul of man.**

This unity of external and internal, movement and stillness, was taken into account in the concept of awakening, which is about the disappearance of the external, objective world. The world disappears only as the external world, and not as the world in itself; it is discovered that the world is a holographic projection of the divine consciousness. That is the true meaning of the 'disappearance of the world'. It also disappears with the disappearance of all the opposites which constitute the experience of the objective world, and that emerge as a consequence of the fundamental opposition between the subject and the object, 'I' and everything 'else'. The subject actually disappears, and with it the objective world that only the subject can project. **The external world is just a contrast of a subjective state.** When the consciousness of the subject was limited by the body, mind and ego, then the objective world of individual shapes existed. When the consciousness of itself becomes pure and awake, on the level of the higher mind and consciousness of the soul, then subjectivity of consciousness disappears and only objective consciousness is left - and that is the soul or the divine consciousness that enables existence itself. Then the subject becomes objective, as the place in which the consciousness of objective existence of itself is crystallized. With such consciousness, he remains what-he-is, the whole of existence which has until then merely used an individual body as the only suitable place for conscious subjects to acquire the finest experiences of itself. Those finest experiences mature when the consciousness in the subject is manifested as pure love and kindness, as a higher understanding.

When in this way the consciousness of existence, through the soul, returns to the divine source, existence has realized its purpose. That is another way of saying that the world disappears, or that we are not identified with existence. The disappearance of the world of objects and cessation of identification with the world is the same as self-realization of the final purpose of the world, through us. If existence exists with the purpose to be conscious or perceived, then it is logical that it cannot continue to exist in the same way when this is achieved. If the purpose of existence is made conscious only through a conscious subject, an awakened man, then it is logical that the world of objects disappears only for that man, in his realization. For all the other unconscious people there is still the world of objects, which they maintain with their unconsciousness.

When man awakens and connects his consciousness with the objective essence of existence (*akasha*), he brings unmanifested nature (*akasha*) into a manifested state; he actualizes it into events and life as we know it. In such a way, an awakened man realizes existence until the end; he makes a full circle and manifests through himself the deepest essence of the quantum field of nature, all its possibilities; everything that is potential becomes actual and creative through him. Consequently, through an awakened man, nature becomes whole and completely realized. That is why it is logical that it cannot exist in the manner it did prior to this moment, in an incomplete and unrealized form.

Together with all of this, the cessation of time also occurs, because time only exists as a space for projecting events, necessary for reasoning and understanding events in general.

Rűpa-dhyânam is related to the individual purification of consciousness from all the precipitations of conditionality of subjective experiences. Here man, through discipline and conscious effort has concluded who he really is in the absolute sense - the subject becomes objectively aware of itself. When this is done to a sufficient extent, when man has made the being conscious, spontaneous purification of insight into the essence of being, the universe and what enables both existence and awareness occurs. Man is faced with the truth of what the being itself is, in the absolute sense, independent of any shape (rűpa) of existence. What he discovered in himself, during the restful phase, now he recognizes in the outer world, in everything, in action. Facing this ultimate perception is why it is called arűpa-dhyânam, the formless contemplation which unbinds and frees man from everything that deceives the presence of the divine consciousness, that makes it together in the world. This is the contemplation in which everything shaped (*rűpa*) is overcome and disappears, and we discover the reason behind everything that is happening - transcendental consciousness of the soul of the man. In correct mindfulness (*samadhi*) 'the old', natural man dies. In *arűpa-dhyânam* the new, spiritual man is born as the embodiment of freedom, which generates everything into existence.

With the disappearance of 'the old man' the world we knew up to that moment also disappears, and with 'the new man,' a new world arises. This is the world of pure divine presence, in which every moment is eternal and every shape is the living expression of endless freedom.

Before *arúpa-dhyânam* man was an individual within an endless whole. Five degrees of *arúpa-dhyânam* show how the individual permanently disappears and only an endless whole remains - but this time not impersonally, as it was, but with all the characteristics of individuality and personality. The individual becomes the embodiment of the divine presence that enables everything. When man's personality disappears into the divine consciousness, it enables the divine consciousness to become an individual and personality. In other words, absolute and relative, external and internal stop being a game of duality for man, and they reveal themselves in his experience as one, as he himself is.[19]

For the successful transition from the old to the new, it is necessary, after the realized calmness in *rúpa-dhyânam*, to participate freely in daily activities up to one hour a day. Alternating rest and activity phases will induce the necessary transformation; one should not fixate on only one extreme. Without participation in activities, the rest itself would be a mere annulment and deadening of life. Also, activity itself without resting in absorption (*dhyânam*) would deprive you of perspective, meaning and spiritual outcome, the unconscious element of nature. The rest brings consciousness and the presence of the divine into activity which, on the other hand, revives the divine and actualizes it in man and the world. Only

---

[19] This exists in the form of a hint in esoteric Christianity, in terms that the Father and Son are one in the Holy Spirit.

with the stronghold that rest provides can the being move towards freedom. Without it, it keeps moving in its own closed circle.

In order for the divine consciousness to completely actualize in man's being, it is not necessary to do anything but to be still, to calm all the activities of nature, the body, feelings and the mind. Then, the shaping of nature into different contents stops and the unconditionality of the divine soul that enables everything is manifested. That is why this ultimate realization is called contemplation without any shaping, or arűpa-dhyânam.

Arűpa-dhyânam has five degrees.

1. The translation of Buddha's speech about the first degree reads as follow: *When a monk completely overcomes the ideas of shapes, when suppressed ideas disappear, when he distracts his attention from the ideas of diversity, then he reaches the realization that space is unlimited and that he resides in the area of spatial limitlessness (akasanancayatanam). With such focus of attention, the ascetic permeates, clears, silences and frees the mind*

Immediately upon ending the absorption (*dhyânam*), we perceive that calm consciousness remains independently present in us, while the body itself moves to stand after the practice of meditation. If we maintain inner silence during this movement after sitting, we can see that the body belongs to the unity of the surrounding space (*prakrti*) and nature's general movement; it does not belong to us. The body in relation to us is the same as the clothes we wear, the objects we touch; the consciousness of our essence or soul was independent from all of this during sitting, and remains so afterward. It is only owing to the fact that we keep the independent consciousness of the soul during the movement and action after meditation that we can see all the existing shapes of causal happening of the world around us are just different modifications of the same space (*akasha*) of nature.

In meditation we have come to the quantum consciousness of *akasha*; that is why immediately after meditation we can spontaneously keep the same quantum consciousness and see the true nature of everything on the finest level - that is, that everything is a manifestation of the unique quantum field. We see that all shapes of our body and all things that make up the world are nothing for themselves, but are the manifestation of the whole of nature, and that essentially the only thing that exists is endless space. **Here, consciousness that we are fully realized occurs, in our essence; we never move or act, but the world (prakrti) moves and acts all around us; we have always been the immovable centre (soul or purusha), the witness of all events.**

This is the first experience of merging pure consciousness of the higher mind with the finest state of nature, ether (*akasha*). In their quantum essence, ether, frequencies of natural events are stationary because they reflect the complete (spherical) holographic unity. Hence the impression of internal immovability in the awakening of consciousness of the soul, while all the rougher manifested physical phenomena move vectorially (transversally). The state of tranquility of transcendental consciousness is non-Hertzian, a stationary state of being. In the first degree of *arūpa-dhyânam*, the perception of reality is experienced in this way only through movement of the body; all the rest of the world moves and turns around us, and we are in our essence immobile, and therefore more conscious.

From the second to the fifth degree of arūpa-dhyânam, this same reality continues to reveal itself, and deepens; feelings and thoughts move and happen as natural phenomena, and we are in our essence immobile and therefore, more aware than these feelings and thoughts are.

This insight is not related solely to movement of the body. Correct meditation (*dhyânam*) brings us to the clear insight that we are neither our body, nor our feelings and thoughts, but the space in which the body, feelings and thoughts arise. We enable them. **We are the wider whole that enables everything. We are always outside of everything we are aware of - it is only because of this that consciousness is possible at all.**

When the fifth degree of *arūpa-dhyânam* is completely realized, during the unification of our consciousness with *akasha*, complete and final perception of nature occurs - a complete differentiation of the soul in nature and existence, and complete realization of the existence of the transcendental divine consciousness which enables everything, through man.

In meditation (*dhyânam*) this was only ever an inner insight and cognition. Here in *arūpa-dhyânam*, it is a concrete transition, a permanent transformation of the whole being, the real death of the 'old man'. This transition is gradually deepened and finally realized in the following degrees of *arūpa-dhyânam*. In the first degree, spatial shaping is realized, and in the other degrees all other shapings are recognized in a similar fashion, up to the higher and more subtle shapes of events in nature and our being.

Man's soul is in this way liberated from the attractive effect of all special phenomena that do not have support in themselves, that are non-existent and transient; and therefore attachment to them leads to loss and pain.

Man widens and reduces his attention, from all special shapes and movements to a wider whole or context (gestalt), to the infinite space that produces all shapes and movements. In this way all shapes and movements are nullified and only space remains real. Then we do not experience the birth of our body as our own birth, but as a spatial modification of nature. We were neither born nor will we die, we are just asleep in one bodily modification of nature, and this dream of individual existence and reality we experience only because of our identification with it. Now we are truly waking up from our imagination, because we see that everything is just nature. With the very act of seeing this, we also see that it is not ours. In the first *arűpa-dhyânam* we definitively perceive that **we are not even born in the body, but we have, as an individual soul and emanation of the divine consciousness, incarnated in nature itself, and the body is in indissoluble unity with all of nature; the body does not exist as an individual being, and only the space of one universal being exists.**

With such cognition of infinite space (*akasha*), man permeates, clears, and silences the mind and frees the soul. Then he notices that all the worries that arose on the basis of special shapes and events of one ostensible body have disappeared, that all these shapes are empty, that they are nothing by themselves or for themselves, and that the remainder is only infinite space.

2. The translation of the original text of this degree reads as follows: *When the monk completely overcomes the area of spatial limitlessness, then he reaches the realization that the consciousness is limitless and resides in the area of limitless consciousness (vinnanancayatanam). With such* *focus of attention the monk permeates, clears, silences and frees the mind.*

When the soul is purified for the presence of unique and infinite space (the quantum field), as the only source and fundamental reality of everything, we realize that the awareness of infinite space is its essential factor. Each special shape, as a modification of limitless space, is information that shapes conscious insight in the subject – in the same way that the cause of the occurrence of the new shape is in nature objective. Modifications of the mind are the finest modifications of the same space that makes everything else. Phenomena are the finest form and framework of all the happenings of nature in space. There, in a conscious subject, the happenings of all shapes purposefully turn to their outcome, summing up the experience or knowledge (*jnana*) of nature. Here one understands that thoughts and states of consciousness are neither a personal creation nor the property of the subject, but the finest phenomena of nature. Here we clearly see that thoughts in our mind move constantly, in creation of the world and events, and that we are in our essence immobile – which makes us more alert and aware of the nature of thoughts, in an objective manner.

In the second degree of *arūpa-dhyânam*, we become conscious of how the essence of *akasha* or spatial shaping of everything takes place in the highest dimension of nature, in the element of air, in the sphere of thoughts or ideas, and how thoughts and ideas shape *akasha*, space - how thoughts arise as vibrations of the quantum field. And thoughts are that: the finest vibrations which spring from the quantum field itself. That is why the element of air is higher than ether or *akasha*.

Thoughts and consciousness represent the state of the relationship between subjects and all entities in local space-time, on their finest level: as information. The subject is only a gathering point of the meaning of phenomena; within the subject, space-time is compressed towards its outcome, and that compression collects information of all shaped events so that, following the principle of conversion (in the same way stars are born), the maximum concentration of information produces the light of experience regarding them. In this manner, nature illuminates itself, it designs itself. Its compression is done under the attractive action of pure unconditionality, the soul in man, and consciousness is only an expression of its proximity, and not a characteristic of nature.

In other words, one perceives here the outcome of all of space, and that is its vibratory area in the form of information; the infinite space creates an informational core, an origination, *a conscious subject*, with the aim not to be impersonal, but to become a personality; and that means that its awareness of itself is expressed in the most concrete way, completely designed and differentiated. *As the subject does not exist without the space in which it resides, in the same way space cannot exist without the subject who is aware of it.* The importance of a conscious subject is actualized here: his perception or awareness is the essence or the fundamental factor in shaping everything in nature.

While in the spatiality of objective nature (*akasha*), shapes cause new events, in the subject this flow of space-time is bent and accelerates, and is compressed into information, moving towards its outcome of conscious realization and completion of the entire torrent of being. We can see that space itself (*akasha*) or the whole of nature shapes cognition of itself in a subject; this informational, thinking, consciousness is the essence of nature, and the world views itself as the whole that it gets acquainted with through us. We can see that consciousness is the identification (*nama*) of the shapes (*rūpa*) of existence, and that is why it is not separate from those shapes – they have a mutually determining influence on each other. The objects of sight, hearing, feeling and mental recognition are not separate from the act of seeing, listening, feeling and the act of recognition. The shapes create the eye, sounds - the ear. That is why man is conscious and awake only when he is present in what is happening, and not when he wonders about what has been, what is, or what will be. Only in such wakefulness is the being shown as it is, as the man's Self. The one who knows does not exist without what is being known. They are the same whole, so there is no subject. In the final outcome, the whole itself is a subject, and for that reason it is endless. **We can have this cognition because we overcome the one who knows, and everything that is known.** This is the essence of this second degree of *arūpa-dhyânam*.

Previously we have seen that our body, shapes and movements are not 'ours', but are modifications of endless space. Now we realize that our individual consciousness is not 'ours', but the outcome of spatial happening for information - the establishing of oneself. **We realize that consciousness of existence in us is possible only because we are not that existence.** We overcome it, transcend it, and the very transcendental position of our soul enables the appearance of the world. **If the conscious subject were not already transcendental, there would not be a conscious subject, nor would there be an objective world.**

With this insight, all worries that arise on the basis of endless space and its forms of manifestation no longer exist. They are worthless and empty, and now only presence in unlimited consciousness is real, as a transcendental subject, as the witness and outcome of all phenomena.

With such presence in pure consciousness, whose transcendentality enables insight into the whole and unity of existence, man permeates, clears, and calms the mind and frees the soul.

3. The translation of the original text reads as follows: *When the monk completely overcomes the area of unlimited consciousness, then he reaches the realization that there is nothing, and he resides in the area of nothing (akincannayatanam). With such focus of attention, the monk permeates, clears, silences and frees the mind.*

Afterwards, having seen that consciousness determines the appearance of the world and the interdependence of information and shapes, that they are the same and only the mind differentiates them, man reaches the emptiness of the world - nothingness. With perfect consciousness, the world is known as it is: it is nothing by itself or for itself. **When the consciousness is calm, the world disappears. Consciousness sets the world in motion.** There is no objective world independent of consciousness - consciousness is the outcome of the objective world. When a conscious man is unconditionally present as pure wakefulness, without thought, the world is nothing by itself - because it is discovered as our inner self (then the essence of existence, *akasha*, finds its outcome in the consciousness of the soul). The world becomes 'something' outside of us only when consciousness, with thoughts, participates by abandoning the presence at the essence of its being. The world is 'something' objective only for the man who exists so that the world is substantial and real to him - for the unconscious man, who is preoccupied with the contents of his consciousness (thoughts), as if they were real in themselves. The world is as real as the thought of the world.

In other words, the world has never existed as an objective entity or problem; the objective world as we know it exists only as our imagination, while on the outside, as the world that's outside of our subjectivity, there is only the unconditioned divine spirit ('living God'; the Absolute); objective nature is simply its holographic imagination, the dream with which it gets awakened through man. The divine consciousness does not awaken because it does not sleep; it is said that it is manifested **through man, through nature**, that is all just an actualization of the divine presence, nothing else. That is why the man who recognizes the divine sees the world only as a divine manifestation. For a calm and awakened man, the world disappears, because he becomes one with it (his consciousness and *akasha* become one, manifested and unmanifested nature become one). When man is in complete unity with the whole, with the cosmos, in pure consciousness without thought, then he cannot see anything outside of himself as something else, or special. To him everything is nothing, because he is all, his essence is all. As the eye cannot see itself, so the awakened cannot see the objective world, because the whole of the world has become its awakened essence, its actualization.

Calm consciousness, in this third degree of arūpadhyânam, enables man to reside in the area of nothing, and with that he permeates, clears, and calms the mind and liberates his soul. For him, all the worries that arise from consciousness and the objective world disappear, because he realizes that all contents of consciousness are empty, and therefore all objects are empty.

4. The translation of this degree reads as follows: *When the monk completely overcomes the area of nothing, then he reaches the area of neither-perception-nor-non-per-*

ception and resides in that area (neva-sanna-nasan-nayatanam). *With such focus of attention the monk permeates, clears, silences and frees the mind.*

And then, having seen that nature is not objective but that it is in itself, at its base, ether, empty (*sunyam*), pure energy where non-Hertzian frequencies represent thoughts, and that their only attractor is the consciousness of our essence or soul, we come to neither-perception-nor-non-perception, at an even higher plane.

It is a state above the dualism of existence and non-existence of thoughts, existence and non-existence of the world. Here, the differentiation of consciousness of the soul is finalized, so every doubt (even the slightest) regarding the true nature of the outcome of existence disappears; that is, all of nature, and nothing more can deceive the pure consciousness of the soul and its divine source.

It overcomes the dualism of consciousness and unconsciousness and world-nothing, and leads to the abandonment of thinking or attempting to fathom reality, existence and non-existence. Even the pure consciousness of ourselves cannot deceive us. Here, after the insight that the outer is our inner, we completely stop participating in the world as an individual, because we dissolve into what enables all individuals.

Having seen that we can be either calm within ourselves, completely awake and independent to such a degree that the objective world disappears, or actively project our consciousness into the objective world and participate in it as the true reality (like in a dream), **we see that both of these possibilities are the same, and that is why we abandon the dualism which conditions us,** and we reside in the area of neither-perception-nor-non-perception of reality as the true home of consciousness of the soul that overcomes the perception of the world as well as the non-perception (nothing); this is where the world never appears, so it can never disappear. *If a being has never been objective and substantial, then nothingness cannot exist, because there was nothing to disappear in the first place.*

Then we realize that everything in the area of the mind and its projections of the world are empty, as is everything else that is in the domain of 'nothing' (created through the disappearance of a projection of the mind. This is nature (*prakrti*), compressing into timeless consciousness of itself and spreading into the time of the object world; this 'something' and 'nothing' are mutually conditioned in the same way as movement and rest, and higher reality is the sojourn beyond their intermittent shifting.

Only then are we permanently always awake to the divine consciousness that is independent from perception and non-perception, stillness and activity, from each dualism that enables consciousness or unconsciousness, existence or non-existence. With this, we overcome the natural shift of conditions which determined when wakefulness is present. Because, here, our wakefulness is what enables both movement and resting, consciousness and unconsciousness, the world and the absence of the world.

Having ascertained that the body and its actions are not our property but the property of nature (*prakrti*), and that the individual consciousness is also not our own, but the outcome of spatial movement of life energy, and finally that individual consciousness (ego) determines what the world is and what it is not (the first three degrees of *arūpa-dhyânam*), we come to the insight that nothing is ours, and is only the product of previous modifications.

Here we see that the unconditionality of the divine presence is not nothingness, the absence of unconsciousness or non-being, just because it overcomes each shape of being and consciousness; but it is the outcome of existence in general, of both being and non-being. We see that we can be free both from being and non-being, from consciousness and unconsciousness, because our soul is behind all these possibilities. Their intermittent shifting, of which we have already been convinced, shows us the transcendental nature of the divine soul in us, which is independently present because it overcomes all states, as a witness: conscious and unconscious states, reality and the dreams, eternalism of substantiality and nothingness. With it we see that the world was not something by itself, able to disappear into nothing just like that, as this 'nothing' also depends on the manifested world; 'nothing' does not exist by itself.

In this degree, we recognize ourselves as independent from all phenomena, from the conscious and unconscious, in reality and in a dream, and for the first time we are awake during a deep sleep without dreams. Here our wakefulness is no different from the essence of nature, the stationary, spherical *akasha*, because it completely recognizes it, to the end; our wakefulness stops moving (vector-like) towards objects and remains outside of space-time.

Experiencing the area of neither-perception-nor-non-perception, as the only unconditioned reality, we overcome all worries that could be realized or have remained unrealized; everything is irrelevant compared to the unconditionality of the soul that is only present, which we are ourselves. 'Everything is irrelevant' means that everything exists only because of the experience of consciousness of the soul; everything that existed was only the holographic imagination of the divine soul, to itself, for the crystallization of consciousness regarding all possibilities of personal existence. If the divine soul is completely self-aware, because it is the source of consciousness, then no imagination is possible anymore, no apparition of any other existence but itself. All of the 'other', the entire cosmos and life, is the divine soul within itself.

5. The translation of the original text reads as follows: *When the monk completely overcomes the area of neither-perception-nor-non-perception, then he resides in the reach of the cessation of perception and in samadhi.*

And then, not paying attention to the dualism of world/nothing, nor to the overcoming of that dualism as neither-perception-nor-non-perception, we see that the presence of unconditioned divine presence can be realized only in the focus of attention without contents, **through six areas of senses of our body**. The human body - and nowhere else - is the only suitable place for this and there is nothing else to be done. And that means here and now, in the actual being as it is. **All previous insights here become concretely realized as our existence; they stop being insights only.** Then everything that was previously known disappears as irrelevant, and the focus of attention is connected only to the presence of unconditioned divine consciousness in the body and its merciful and tender **manifestation through six areas of senses**. With that we realize the highest responsibility for existence. *The unconditionality that enables the world and life now stops being abstract and becomes a concrete living reality, with its own body and senses; the reality that breathes and acts as our being. Then the void becomes the shape, and the* *shape becomes void. Then the divine consciousness becomes man, and man becomes the divine presence.*

Theologically speaking: the kingdom of heaven then truly exists on earth, as well as in the sky - through the man. In no other way can this ideal be realized but through man.[20]

Finally, we come to the big awakening, when for the first time we see everything from the perspective of the soul, and we realize that everything *coming from mind, both consciousness and unconsciousness of self*, everything that has been achieved and realized as new, and even the awake presence of the divine consciousness described here, is only an unstable and transient phenomenon, an event of nature (*prakrti*), its purification, and not consciousness of the soul, because it has always been awake, free and independent. It has never been any different. We are never able to get the highest consciousness that we discover in 'the final awakening', because it represents what we always are and have always been, and what we could never lose. Upon awakening we discover that there actually is no awakening, because there is no sleep; everything is one and the same divine consciousness that recognizes itself. This, in other words, means that nothing objective is happening. Everything was just

---

[20] The myth of the second coming of Christ can only be properly understood if we accept Christ as the embodiment of perfect man through whom the divine presence can be manifested. That is why the coming of Christ actually means the coming of the perfect man, through which will also come the divine presence. Esoteric Christianity considers Christ to be the archetype of man's essence, the Self, in the sense in which Meister Eckehart said: "Who is the Son of God? Every good man is the son of God" (Meister Eckehart: Deutsche Predigten und Traktate; Carl Hanser Verlag, München, 1963).

the game of perception of One and the same, and not the achievement or realization of something new.

We have not achieved anything new with this complete awakening, but we have discovered what we have always been. Nothing objectively happens or changes. We realize the authenticity of an unconditioned human soul, always free and independent, with insight into the causality and unity of nature (prakrti) - through the fact that all material phenomena are interconnected and subordinate to the laws of physics (from the subatomic to the cosmic) and that clearly shows that absolutely nothing new happens in the world, and that everything is One. The causality of nature connects everything into One.

Only when consciousness of the soul identifies itself with a consciousness individually modified by the mind is that identification projected for that soul as "the world" and "events". Modifications of consciousness under the influence of the mind give name and shape to every event. Outside these modifications of the mind, there are no happenings, because everything is in accordance with the law of causality of nature, i.e. all is One. Everything that exists and manifests itself from nature already existed in it, in *akasha*, as a possibility. Everything that can happen in general, the potential of everything, already exists in the unity of nature, in the quantum field. **An individual mind is only focused on individual possibilities and they are actualized.** The mind only actualizes the possibilities that already exist in the universal field of nature. **That is why there is a need for an individual mind: to attract individual phenomena from the universal quantum field. Individuality creates individuality, as in a mirror.** Everything already exists, but to us, from our subjective point of view, it appears as something new is happening. However, **nothing real is actualized outside of the** *mind*. Everything is already as the divine Absolute and there is nothing to be actualized. All actualization is only an illusion of the mind - our dream. ***Awakening is the realization that nothing is happening outside of the mind.***

If nothing is actualized outside of the mind, then the mind/ego is only an illusion the dream is made up of. 'I' and the object world are the same illusions, and mutually supportive. They disappear together upon awakening.

Any separation and the need for merging disappears in awakening. Until the final awakening, this process looks to us like we keep separating ourselves from something unfavourable and enslaving, hoping to master and achieve some state that is liberating and favourable; like a twist from the outer to the inner, from restlessness to calm. All of this is an illusion which disappears upon awakening - which in reality represents only the act of understanding and nothing more. ***The awakening of the soul is its understanding of itself; that is, of what it is, understanding the true nature of existence here and now, and not a separation or achieving some new state.***

* * *

Here all five degrees of *arūpa-dhyanam* are completed.

Having achieved the goal of meditation, with the disclosure of all the illusions of individuality, the mind and ego, the divine consciousness becomes completely discovered through man. Meditation is complete when in man all illusions that anything exists but the divine presence itself disappear. The divine presence is the only reality. It has never been nor could it ever be disturbed, because nothing is possible outside of it. The only thing that was happening was the perfecting of its perception through the human body, existence and life, through the deeds of man. The divine completely recognizes and actualizes itself in this world only through an awakened man, once he consciously turns to himself. This is the purpose of meditation.

The awakened man lives in the divine Absolute here and now, walks and breathes in it, thinks, speaks and acts with it; he recognizes it in everything he sees and touches, as the expression of the divine presence, complete perfection, bliss and love.

Awakening signals the end of the need for meditation. The awakening happens one beautiful day all by itself, spontaneously, suddenly, as the dawning of light and clarity that rises above existence, throughout all dimensions; then everything stops and disappears, all problems, which are only a set design for a big show of drama of our life, everything stops being real and the game of consciousness is over; time disappears and space ceases to be different from our being; behind all these scenes everything is unveiled as the expression of the divine soul and its presence.

It can happen suddenly in the morning, when a man gets up. Or during the day while he is doing something; but it can never happen to someone because he brought it upon himself intentionally. This happens only when man is unable to resist it any longer, and when he completely surrenders, when he himself disappears, his limited individual mind or 'I' ceases to exist - only then can consciousness of his transcendental unborn soul completely break through and manifest in this world, through his body and mind.

Then we die for this world; that is, the world stops being real for us, but due to perfect understanding of all the dimensions of existence and its meaning, owing to the correct meditation which has equally encompassed all dimensions of our being, we continue to live and work as though nothing has happened. Objectively observed, indeed nothing has.

The final awakening is an act of complete surrender. All the effort of meditation is not about striving toward a goal so much as actually resisting it, and overcoming the resistance to awakening and surrendering to the divine, which has always been the only reality, both of ourselves and existence itself. Each human life in this world is composed of resisting reality. Hence the suffering. Meditation is only the complete awareness of that resistance and its cessation. Only with careful awareness can that resistance decrease. We surrender to the divine only when we cannot resist anymore.

Although the awakened man continues to live surrounded by other beings whose attention is turned outwardly to the seeming oblivion of themselves, beings who still live in an illusory conflict with themselves and with the divine that enables them, the awakened man is still able to see the divine presence in them, the divine that sleeps like a little child.

He lives among them as an awake man among the sleeping, much like any parent who patiently waits for his child to mature. Parental love and attention is only a reflection of the consciousness of the soul, the way the soul views this world and the people inhabiting it. If parental love would spread through the entire world, as the principle of social order, this world would be heaven.

SUMMARY OF THE PRACTICE OF MEDITATION

Everyday practice of meditation should be as follows:
- Getting up at six o'clock in the morning (after sleeping of 6 to 8 hours).
- Doing the morning exercises from *hatha-yoga* 'Sun Salutation' (*surya namaskar*) or the Tibetan exercises for rejuvenation.[21]
- Sitting in meditation of tranquility (*za zen* or *rŭpa-dhyânam*) for at least 20 minutes, and with experience longer; it is not necessary for more than one hour.
- The same exercise of yoga and meditation of tranquility should be repeated in the evening, at sunset.
- After the practice of mental tranquility, the exercise of the focus of attention should follow suit spontaneously (*satipatthâna*) and with insight (*vipassana*), step by step (movement of the body, feelings, general state of the mind). The practice of awareness should be made part of everyday work and routine. Work and all activities should be the subject of the focus of attention and awareness. We should not adjust our activities and work responsibilities to suit attention and awareness, but conversely, awareness should be adjusted to work and activities. However, whenever possible, we should slow down movement and strengthen consciousness of the body,

---

[21] Peter Kelder – Fountain of Youth – Tibetan exercises for rejuvenation ("Ancient Secret of the Fountain of Youth"). It is certainly desirable and healthy to do complete *hatha-yoga*, but it is not necessary.

feelings and states of mind. In the beginning, certain parts of practicing attention should be separated and practiced individually, until we perfect them. For example, one week we should practice only awareness of the body, the next week only awareness of feelings, the next only the general states of mind etc., in order to be able to connect them all into the overall awareness of the entire being. While practicing, beginners can establish in themselves the thought: "In me now is such-and-such state of consciousness" - towards the body, feelings and mind. The entire exercise is about the practice of witnessing, establishing objectivity, and not judging.

- Occasionally, throughout the year, we should go on a multiday practice of intensive meditation, performed in some Buddhist monastery or community of open type that practices Buddhist meditation.

***

The entire practice of meditation should follow once certain preconditions are met, including healthy and moderate living and nutrition. Nutrition should be vegan, and for those who are unable to follow this dietary regime, it can be 80% vegan and raw food, and 20% processed, eliminating foods proven to be toxic. Moderate fasting is the best for meditation.

No psychoactive drugs and substances should be ingested. Their effect is opposite to the effect of meditation.

There should be a permanent space for meditation in which you will not be disturbed by noise and people who do not meditate.

The practice of meditative absorption (*rŭpa-dhyânam*) is performed in the sitting position; the back must be upright, but not stiff. The body in meditation will be upright and relaxed with the help of imagination: visualize that the top of your head is hanging from the ceiling, as if hung. The lower part of the back can be leaning against something, but the back must remain upright with legs crossed; it is desirable to be in the lotus position on the surface where we sit, but not necessary; legs can be crossed on the floor while we sit on something, for example a chair; hands are clasped in the lap, left in right, with palms up, thumbs connected; sight should be lowered down the nose line, in the direction of the floor in front of the body, and diffuse, looking into space, without focusing on one point. It is best to turn towards a wall, so the mind will not deal with anything it sees ahead. We start by making breathing conscious, following the surface of the entire body, especially the whole head where all the thoughts and mind are involved. Consciousness in the beginning of meditation should always move behind each thought, always a witness and objective, neutrally perceiving each movement of the mind, vision or feeling. This witnessing and turning always behind is experienced only as increasing self-consciousness, as the turning to oneself, increasing the presence in oneself, here and now, in existence itself. The goal of meditation is that this consciousness remains without contents, no different from existence. Then, its only characteristic is pure wakefulness. The goal of meditation is that existence is awakened more than ever before.

It is of crucial importance to practice mediation in the morning. By doing so we break away from the unconscious relaxation and passivity of the sleeping process. If we get up in the morning and start the day without meditation, we continue the subconscious passivity we had during sleep. Our dreaming phase does not always end in the morning when we wake up. For the greater part, we go on dreaming in our aware phase. That is why people are unconscious when they are awake, they remain irrational, conditioned and mechanical in their activities. When we meditate in the morning we create a gap, an interruption in the flow of our passive happenings from the world of dreaming, much like restarting a computer; we introduce true awareness into our actions in the real world. It is a big illusion to think that we are awake when we get out of bed in the morning. Meditation is the only true awakening. It is imperative, too, to finalize the day with meditation; we annul the passivity and mechanicality we gathered throughout the day and we go to sleep liberated from conditioning. Such consciousness may continue during lucid dreaming.

After the morning exercise and meditation, one should go and do everything that needs to be done, objectively, not avoiding anything and not imposing anything because of meditation, keeping the awareness of witnessing opposed to everything that exists, like in meditation. Everyday work should be our preparation for meditation in practice, and meditative absorption should be the preparation for conscious work. All in all, we should be a witness to the feeling that we are doing something (nature, or prakrti, does everything, we are only conscious because everything keeps happening, the conscious subject around which everything is spinning). That is also connected and interdependent: the awareness that we are merely a witness of this work, and that we are neither the body nor the mind that is working, is directly connected and depends on accepting any work or experience, no matter what. We should not avoid anything, just as we should not attach to anything. That is 'presence in the present moment,' which is at the same time complete independence of transcendental consciousness of the soul

(Self, Atman) from everything that is happening in that moment. There is no presence in reality of the present moment without independence, because there is no consciousness without independence. Participating in events and independence from these events must become one and equal. That is because the consciousness in its essence is transcendental, above everything it awakens. If it were not above, it would not be able to be aware of anything.

From other types of recreation that support meditation, solar yoga comes highly recommended; gazing at the sun, according to the instructions from Hira Ratan Manek and an advanced course in *solar yoga* with instructions from Sunyogi Umasankar (sunyoga.info). As much time as possible should be spent in nature, and as little as possible in urban environments which influence the consciousness negatively and in a conditioning way.

The only warning which can be given about meditation is the following: the practice of meditation will bring a deepening of consciousness, becoming aware of everything that was unconscious, up to a point of increased sensitivity and intuition. With this, it will bring to the surface everything that was unconscious, everything that was suppressed and disturbed, and these issues will start automatically to unveil and upgrade in the light of consciousness. We should know that it will happen, and be prepared. It is known that meditation will cause some reactions in us. Depending on the contents, these reactions can be manifested in the form of visions, memories, thoughts, bodily sensations and pains, or in the form of external events and interpersonal relationships. You should not allow this to pull you away from the correct attention which is pure witnessing of everything. This is only a process of purification. It can be more difficult or easier, faster or more lasting, depending on the individual life experience and karma. In any case, these reactions of awareness and cleansing the suppressed contents in us are the main cause of turning away from proper meditation and stopping with the practice entirely. This is the main cause of 'difficulties in meditation' which beginners experience. When the subconsciousness is made aware of, such difficulties will not be manifested on the outside as such, but they will be manifested through the subconsciousness itself, through ourselves, through our mind, as the illusion of a 'lack of will for meditation' and different justifications which we give ourselves to stop - that 'it is not for us' or that it is difficult, or we should adjust meditation to ourselves, to try to find 'some easier meditation'. In meditation we should always adjust ourselves to it, not adjust meditation to us. That is the purpose of discipline.

The only right thing to do is to use all such states of mind and to make them the subject of meditation, of the aware. To use Buddha's words here, your personal experience should be your only criterion; there is no need to take into account anything else.

It is easy to notice that the instructions for meditation given here are completely objective and purified from any ideology, mental conditioning and manipulation. This is pure mental hygiene. Therefore, any other type of meditation is a form of conditioning and manipulation.

An additional problem remains that there are people who are so mentally conditioned and manipulated that it is not possible to easily set themselves free from conditioning, in the way the practice of meditation is presented on these pages. To them, for therapeutic reasons it is necessary to gradually reduce and abolish their forms of conditioning, in order to come to the pure mental hygiene and objective consciousness that is achieved with the meditation described here. However, such a problem requires elaborate explanation which would be, and is, the subject of other books, professional advice and therapies. Nevertheless, everyone can judge for themselves about how close they are to the final and pure meditation, in the way described here, and how much maturity is still required.

We all undergo various states of consciousness and emotions. These changes can be short-lived and barely noticeable, but also long-term and taking several seconds to several hours or days to manifest. The roots of these problems may be of the inner kind, such as karmic maturity and health, or of the outer kind, in the form of living conditions and circumstances created by us or somebody else. However, all the states of consciousness and all emotional states have two things in common: they are of transient nature, and we are the living witnesses to all of them. We are always behind all states and all emotions, and we can be aware of them. The problem is in the power of our testimony, because it is weak, our self-consciousness is weak, and various states of mind or emotional states tend to overpower our self-consciousness, forcing us to identify with them. Only when they get weaker do we become aware that we have identified with their contents. Only when we wake up do we realize what happened.

All the emotional and mental problems that make meditation seem hard are easily overcome by recapitulation, by exploiting the two facts we have stated: all of these states are of transient nature, and we are always the witness to them. Recapitulation helps us distinguish ourselves from non-ourselves, the consciousness of our soul or the Self, the essence, from the mind which is ever-changing and reacting to outer stimulants. We should simply detect all the alterations in states using recapitulation, memorize the periods of exaltation well, and then with full awareness establish the periods between exaltations, when we are depressed, when our consciousness is narrowed and experiences identification of a lower kind. We should simply connect the dots in recapitulation and find those periods when our mental state was elevated, so that the periods of narrowed consciousness become clear to us. It will secure our position as a witness; the states keep changing, yet we are always the same, we always exist. This is the principle of tantra. We may not pull it off at once, but if we persevere in recapitulation and establishing, the periods of direct insight will become stronger and longer, and the stages of narrowed consciousness will get shorter and weaker. They will be lost in the end, and we will never again experience our unconsciousness and the loss of our true nature.

This will be an additional method in overcoming the emotional or mental difficulties that interfere with our meditation. Meditation is a direct road leading to the same goal that all other methods go towards indirectly.

Experience shows that even the most conditioned mind can, with discipline, with the help of the meditation described here, break through to higher states of objective consciousness, no matter how difficult and clumsy the beginning may seem. No matter how good a therapy for healing trauma and emotional blocks is, in the end it is always shown as a bypass method for reaching objective consciousness of the problem, and in reality this is the goal of meditation.[22] The key is only in maintaining firm discipline and trust in intuition that we are on the right path, which comes from consciousness of the soul. Without such inspiration, no one is able to practice meditation. Discipline and inspiration are the only basis for success in meditation.

***

If for any reason, somebody thinks that he/she cannot do the meditation properly in the way described here, or that it is not enough, or right, or that there is still something for him/her left to do, or that some things he/she still does not understand - then he/she should get up before six o'clock.

---

[22] For those who still need some preparation for meditation, I recommend "The Sedona Method: Your Key to Lasting Happiness, Success, Peace and Emotional Well-Being" by Hale Dwoskin.

Printed in Great Britain
by Amazon